Onward, Christian Soldiers

Protestants Affirm the Church

John MacArthur
Joel Beeke
Jonathan Gerstner
Don Kistler
James White
John Armstrong
Donald S. Whitney
R. C. Sproul
Phil Johnson
Joseph E. Pipa
John H. Gerstner

Don Kistler, General Editor

Soli Deo Gloria Publications
. . . for instruction in righteousness . . .

Soli Deo Gloria Publications
P. O. Box 451, Morgan, PA 15064
(412) 221-1901/ FAX 221-1902
www.SDGbooks.com

*

*

ISBN 1-57358-102-X

Contents

Author Profiles   v

Introduction   xi
Dr. Bruce Bickel

I Love Thy Church, O God   1
John MacArthur on the Importance of the Church

Glorious Things of Thee Are Spoken   23
Joel Beeke on the Doctrine of the Church

On the Rock of Ages Founded   68
Jonathan Gerstner on the Marks of a True Church

Blest Be the Tie That Binds   96
Don Kistler on Church Membership

Jesus Shall Reign   107
James White on Authority in the Church

Weep O'er the Erring One, Lift Up the Fallen   131
John Armstrong on Church Discipline

To Her My Toils and Cares Be Giv'n   174
Donald S. Whitney on the Working Church

iii

One O'er All the Earth   206
    R. C. Sproul on Church Unity

We Are Not Divided   226
    Phil Johnson on Denominations and Unity

Great Things He Hath Taught Us   249
    *Joseph E. Pipa on the Importance of Creeds
    and Confessions in the Church*

Guide Me, O Thou Great Jehovah   272
    John Gerstner on When a Person Must Leave a Church

Author Profiles

Dr. John MacArthur is pastor/teacher at Grace Community Church in Sun Valley, California. A graduate of Talbot Theological Seminary, he can be heard daily throughout the country on his radio program, "Grace To You." He is the author of numerous bestsellers, including: *The Gospel According to Jesus, The Vanishing Conscience, Faith Works, Charismatic Chaos,* and his new book on discernment, *Reckless Faith.* Dr. MacArthur also serves as President of the Master's College and Seminary in Southern California. He was a contributing author to the Soli Deo Gloria volumes *Justification by Faith ALONE!, Sola Scriptura,* and *Trust and Obey.*

Dr. Joel Beeke is the pastor of Heritage Netherlands Reformed Congregation of Grand Rapids, Michigan, and President and Professor of Systematic Theology and Homiletics at Puritan Reformed Theological Seminary. He earned a Ph.D. in Reformation and Post-Reformation Theology from Westminster Theological Seminary in Philadelphia. He is the author of numerous books, most recently *The Quest for Full Assurance, A Reader's Guide to Reformed Literature, Reformed Confessions Harmonized* (with Dr. Sinclair Ferguson), and *Knowing and Living the Christian Life.* Dr. Beeke is also editor of *The Banner of Sovereign Grace Truth* magazine, President of Reformation Heritage Books, and radio pastor for "The Gospel Trumpet." He was a contributing author to *Justification by Faith ALONE!, Sola Scriptura,* and *Trust and Obey.*

Dr. Jonathan Gerstner is Professor of Apologetics and Church History at Knox Theological Seminary in Fort Lauderdale, Florida. He received a Ph.D. from the University of Chicago in theology, and has also done graduate study at the University of Utrecht in the Netherlands and the University of Stellensboch in the Republic of South Africa. He is the author of *The Thousand-Generation Covenant: Dutch Reformed Covenant Theology and Group Identity in Colonial South Africa from 1652 to 1814.* He has served as Professor of Systematic and Practical Theology at Payne Theological Seminary in Wilberforce, Ohio (the oldest African-American seminary) and as Executive Secretary of the Reformed Church in Canada (where he was a denominational spokesman and consultant in new church development and church revitalization). He is the son of the late John and Edna Gerstner.

Rev. Don Kistler is the founder and president of Soli Deo Gloria Ministries, Inc. He is the author of

A Spectacle Unto God: The Life and Death of Christopher Love and *Why Read the Puritans Today?* He is also the editor of all the Puritan reprints published by Soli Deo Gloria.

Dr. James White is Scholar-in-Residence in the College of Christian Studies at Grand Canyon University in Arizona and is Adjunct Professor teaching Greek for Golden Gate Baptist Theological Seminary. He holds a bachelor's degree in Bible and a minor in Biblical Greek from Grand Canyon University, where he graduated *Summa Cum Laude* and was a Ray Maben Scholar. He holds a master's degree in theology from Fuller Theological Seminary, Pasadena, California. An ordained Baptist minister, he is the author of seven books including *The Fatal Flaw, Answers to Catholic Claims, Justification by Faith, Letters to a Mormon Elder,* and *The King James Only Controversy.* As the director of Alpha and Omega Ministries, a Christian apologetics ministry based in Phoenix, James has engaged in numerous public debates against the leading Roman Catholic apologists across the nation on subjects such as *sola Scriptura,* the Mass, the Papacy, and justification by faith.

Dr. John Armstrong is the Director of Reformation & Revival Ministries, located in Carol Stream,

Illinois. He was a Baptist pastor for over twenty years before assuming his present position in 1992. He also serves as the editor of *Reformation & Revival Journal* and *Viewpoint,* while conducting an international itinerant speaking ministry. He is the general editor of *Roman Catholicism: Evangelical Protestants Analyze What Unites and Divides Us, The Coming Evangelical Crisis,* and *The Compromised Church.* He is the author of *When God Moves, Preparing for True Revival,* and *Can Fallen Pastors Be Restored?* Dr. Armstrong was also a contributing author to *Justification by Faith ALONE!, Sola Scriptura,* and *Trust and Obey.*

Dr. Donald S. Whitney is Assistant Professor of Spiritual Formation at Midwestern Baptist Theological Seminary in Kansas City, Missouri. A native of Arkansas, and a graduate of Arkansas State University, he earned a Master of Divinity degree from Southwestern Baptist Theological Seminary in Fort Worth, Texas, and a D.Min. from Trinity Evangelical Divinity School in Deerfield, Illinois. Before assuming his present position, he pastored a local church for fifteen years. He is the author of *Spiritual Disciplines for the Christian Life* (NavPress) and *Spiritual Disciplines Within the Church* (Moody Press).

Dr. R. C. Sproul is founder and chairman of Ligonier Ministries in Orlando, Florida. He is an ordained minister in the Presbyterian Church of America, in addition to being Distinguished Visiting Professor of Systematic Theology and Apologetics at Knox Theological Seminary in Ft. Lauderdale, Florida. Dr. Sproul is in constant demand as a speaker and author. He has authored many books, among them *The Holiness of God, Chosen by God, Abortion: A Rational Look at an Emotional Issue,* and *Knowing Scripture.* He was a contributing author to *Justification by Faith ALONE!, Sola Scriptura,* and *Trust and Obey.*

Phil Johnson is the executive director of "Grace to You," a Christian radio and tape ministry featuring the teaching of John MacArthur. An elder at Grace Community Church in Southern California, Phil has edited most of Dr. MacArthur's major books. He is a trustee of the Martyn Lloyd-Jones Recording Trust in England, and teaches courses in writing and editing at The Master's College and Seminary.

Dr. Joseph Pipa, Jr. is the President and Dean of the Faculty of Greenville Presbyterian Theological Seminary in Taylors, South Carolina. He is also Professor of Historical and Systematic Theology.

He holds the Ph.D. degree from Westminster Theological Seminary in Philadelphia. Dr. Pipa pastored local churches for over 25 years before accepting his present position. He is the author of *Root and Branch* and *The Lord's Day*. He has also contributed articles to *The Banner of Truth* magazine.

Dr. John H. Gerstner earned his Ph.D. from Harvard University. He pastored several churches before accepting a professorship at Pittsburgh-Xenia Theological Seminary, where he taught church history for over 30 years. Before his death in 1996, he was a visiting professor at Trinity Evangelical Divinity School in Deerfield, Illinois and adjunct professor at Knox Theological Seminary in Ft. Lauderdale, Florida. He authored many books and articles, among which his *magnum opus* is the three-volume set, *The Rational Biblical Theology of Jonathan Edwards*. He has written numerous books published by Soli Deo Gloria: *Repent or Perish, Theology for Everyman, The ABC's of Assurance, Theology in Dialogue, Primitive Theology, Jonathan Edwards: Evangelist, Jonathan Edwards on Heaven and Hell, Reasons for Faith, Reasons for Duty,* and *John H. Gerstner: The Early Writings* (2 volumes).

Introduction

If we were to inquire of people why they should study and become familiar with the doctrine of the Church, we would most likely discover that the majority of respondents would say that they do not need to at all. Some would, no doubt, express their lack of interest in such an assignment because of their distaste for organizational structures or institutions. Others might say that they have grown up in the church and are familiar enough with its function. There might be those who would want to talk about their views on denominationalism, or those who perceive the church to be merely an edifice. We might also anticipate a segment of respondents who would want to spend time on "more relevant" issues confronting them today. Whatever responses we might gather from such an inquiry, we are quite sure they would be varied.

When pondering such a question from a biblical perspective, it seems quite apparent to us that a lack of interest in the Church would be tantamount to rejecting that which Christ loved and for which He gave Himself (Ephesians 5:25). One of the great weaknesses of this generation of professing believers is a lack of understanding of the person and work of Christ, fostered by a paucity of understanding of the Church He came to gather and to build. Contrary to popular opinion in our culture today, the Church is not an institution created by the religious establishment. According to Scripture, it is a body of people who have been assembled through a call or summons. Additionally, the concept of gathering is not so much focused on having a meeting as it is focused on meeting the One who called the gathering together—God. The purpose of assembling together is to hear His voice.

It is significant to note that the biblical word for church (*ekklesia*) always refers to people, not to buildings. Physical structures are not the Church; they are merely the facility where the Church gathers. Christians do not attend church, we *are* the Church. Thus, in describing this assembly of "called-out ones," the Scriptures use such designations as "the body of Christ," "the bride of Christ," "the Church of God," "the family of God," "the fold of Christ," "God's building," "God's field," "the Lamb's wife," "a spiritual house," and "the New Jerusalem" as synonyms for the universal brotherhood of the redeemed. Because the Church is so closely united to the Lord, we will get to know Him better when we have a better understanding of His Church. It is for this reason that we have published this collection of essays.

Because our noted authors prepared their assigned topics independently of one another, there will inevitably be some repetition with regard to content. We trust that these unplanned repetitions will be used sovereignly by the Holy Spirit as items of emphasis for personal application and growth as you feed on these delicacies of biblical cuisine.

It is our strong conviction that the preoccupation of the Church must be Christ. Jesus did not say, "I will build *your* church." Nor did He say, "You will build *My* church." Rather He said, "*I* will build *My* church." Because it is His Church, we must recommit ourselves to being aggressive responders to what He is doing in His Church. It is not for us to determine, design, or dictate what the Church should be. He has already done that. May God grant you, the reader, and us, the publisher, a clear vision of who He is and what we are to be as His body, and may it be so for His glory.

Dr. Bruce Bickel (Chairman of the Board)
Pittsburgh, PA

The Board of Directors

John Bishop	Don Kistler	Chris Meinzer
Annapolis, MD	Pittsburgh, PA	Pittsburgh, PA
Peter Neumeier	Lance Quinn	Jack Wilson
Powder Springs, GA	Little Rock, AR	Pittsburgh, PA

I love Thy Church, O God!
Her walls before Thee stand,
Dear as the apple of Thine eye
And graven on Thy hand.

Timothy Dwight

I Love Thy Church, O God

John MacArthur on the Importance of the Church

A young man contemplating conversion to Roman Catholicism wrote me to explain why he was thinking of leaving Protestantism: Protestants don't seem to appreciate the Church. The Bible describes the Church as an institution Christ founded and loves. The Church is everything to Catholics; it is nothing to most of my Protestant friends.

In a similar vein, the July 15, 1998 issue of *Christianity Today* included an article by Timothy George, Dean of Beeson Divinity School at Samford University. The article's subtitle: "Responding to the main criticism Catholics have against evangelicals: that we have no doctrine of the church." Dr. George quoted from a sermon by Dietrich Bonhoeffer, in which Bonhoeffer noted that the word "church" to Protestants "has the sound of something infinitely commonplace, more or less indifferent and superfluous, that does not make their heart beat faster; something with which a sense of boredom is so often associated."[1]

Let's be honest: there is too much truth in those

---

[1] "What I'd Like to Tell the Pope about the Church," http://www.christianity.net/ct/8T7/8T7041.html.

criticisms to dismiss them lightly. Evangelicals are far too prone to indifference about the church. Some evangelicals live on the periphery of the church, attending and observing without ever really becoming an integral part of the body. Many who profess faith in Christ remain totally impassive about the church. Author Michael Griffiths noted,

> A high proportion of people who "go to church" have forgotten what it is all for. Week by week they attend services in a special building and go through their particular, time-honored routine, but give little thought to the purpose of what they are doing. The Bible talks about the "the bride of Christ" but the church today seems like a ragged Cinderella. It needs to reaffirm the non-negotiable, essential elements that God designed for it to be committed to.[2]

He's right. Worse yet, I know of people in full-time Christian service, employed by evangelical parachurch organizations, who have no involvement whatsoever with any local church. This is to the shame of the whole evangelical movement.

Of course, the remedy for evangelical apathy about the church is not a return to the twisted, ex-

------

[2] *God's Forgetful Pilgrims* (Grand Rapids, Eerdmans, 1978), p. 37.

trabiblical ecclesiology of the Roman Catholic Church. Evangelical Protestants must approach ecclesiology as they have soteriology, from the perspective of Scripture alone. Unfortunately, even among many Protestants, too many of the popular notions about the Church are laden with human traditions, superstitions, and other holdovers from the medieval Catholic Church. Scripture alone can give us a sound understanding and appreciation of the true role and nature of the Church.

I love the Church. I am an inveterate and incurable lover of the Church. It thrills me beyond expression to serve the Church. Although I am also involved in some parachurch ministries, I wouldn't trade my ministry in the Church for all of them combined. The Church takes first place in my ministry priorities, and all the parachurch ministries I serve are subordinate to, and grow out of, my ministry in the Church. In fact, my whole life has been lived in the church. My father was a pastor, as were my grandfathers for three more generations before him. So a deep love for the Church practically runs in my blood. But here are some biblical reasons why I love the Church:

1. *The Church is being built by the Lord Himself.*

The Church is the New Testament counterpart of the Old Testament temple. I'm not referring to a church building, but the body of all true believers.

It is a spiritual building (1 Peter 2:5), the dwelling-place of the Holy Spirit (1 Corinthians 3:16–17; 2 Corinthians 6:16), the place where God's glory is most clearly manifest on earth, and the proper nucleus and focal point of spiritual life and worship for the community of the redeemed.

God Himself is the architect and builder of this temple. In Ephesians 2:19–22, Paul writes,

> So then you are no longer strangers and aliens, but you are fellow citizens with the saints, and are of God's household, having been built on the foundation of the apostles and prophets, Christ Jesus Himself being the cornerstone, in whom the whole building, being fitted together, is growing into a holy temple in the Lord, in whom you also are being built together into a dwelling of God in the Spirit.

It is impossible to overstate the importance of the Church in the eternal plan of God. The Church is *His* building (1 Corinthians 3:9). Moreover, He is the immutable, sovereign, omnipotent Lord of heaven. His Word cannot return void, but always accomplishes what He says (Isaiah 55:11). He is always faithful and cannot deny Himself (2 Timothy 2:13). His sovereign purposes always come to pass, and His will is always ultimately fulfilled (Isaiah 46:10). His plan is invincible and unshakable, and He will bring to pass all that He has spoken (v. 11). And He has spoken about building the Church in the most triumphant words.

For example, in Matthew 16:18 Christ said, "I will build My church; and the gates of Hades will not overpower it." He who knows His sheep by name (John 10:3), He who wrote their names down before the foundations of the world (Revelation 13:8), personally guarantees that the gates of Hades will not prevail against the Church He is building.

"The gates of Hades" was a Jewish expression for death. Hades is the place of the dead, and the gates of Hades represents the portal into that place—death itself. Hades is also the domain of the devil. Hebrews 2:14 refers to Satan as the one "who had the power of death," and verse 15 says he used that power to keep people in fear and bondage all their lives. But now Christ has broken that power, liberating His people from Satan's dominion—in essence, He has broken down the gates of Hades. And therefore even the power of death—the strongest weapon Satan wields—cannot prevent the ultimate triumph of the Church He is building.

There's still more significance to the imagery of "the gates of Hades." Gates are a walled city's most vital defensive safeguards. Christ's words therefore portray the Church militant, storming the very gates of hell, victoriously delivering people from the power of death. Thus Christ assures the triumph of the Church's evangelistic mission. *He* is building the Church, and the work will not be thwarted.

Christ's promise in this passage should not be misconstrued. He does not suggest that any particular church will be infallible. He does not teach that any of the bishops of the church will be error-free. He does not guarantee that this or that individual church will not apostatize. He does not promise success and prosperity to every congregation. But He does pledge that *the Church*—that universal body of believers under Christ's headship, the spouse, the body, and the fullness of Him who fills all in all—will have a visible being and a testimony in this world as long as the world itself shall last. All the enemies of truth combined shall never secure the defeat or destruction of the Church.

Notice also that the Church is a work in progress. Christ is still building His Church. We are still being joined together (Ephesians 2:21). The Church is still under construction (v. 22). God is not finished yet. The imperfections and blemishes in the visible church are still being refined by the Master Builder.

And here's something remarkable: The plan for the finished product is a blueprint that was drawn in eternity past.

2. The Church Is the outworking of an eternal plan.

In Titus 1:2, the Apostle Paul writes of the "eternal life which God, who cannot lie, *promised before time began*" (New King James Version, emphasis added). In this context, the Apostle Paul was describing his ministry, a ministry of evangelism and salvation "for the faith of those chosen of God," the church (v. 1).

And as Paul describes his ministry, he outlines God's redemptive purpose, from election ("those chosen of God," v.1), to salvation ("the knowledge of the truth," v. 1), to sanctification ("which is according to godliness," v. 1), to final glory ("in the hope of eternal life," v. 2). All of this is *God's* work (cf. Romans 8:29–30), something He "promised before time began."

In other words, in eternity past, before anything was created, *before time began,* God determined to begin and to finish His redemptive plan. People were chosen. Their names were written down that they might be brought to faith, to godliness, and to glory. God *promised* this before time began.

To whom did God make the promise? This was before time, and therefore before creation. So there weren't any people or angels around; and even if angels had been created, they do not participate in redemption. So to whom, then, did God make this promise?

We find the answer in 2 Timothy 1:9. There we read that God "saved us and called us with a holy calling, not according to our works, but according to His own purpose and grace which was given to us in Christ Jesus before time began" (NKJV). That verse ends with the same phrase we find in Titus 1:2: "before time began." And here the apostle says that God's eternal purpose—this same promise that was made before the beginning of time—"was given to us in Christ Jesus." The eternal pledge of our salvation involved a promise made by the Father to the Son before time began.

This is a staggering reality. In the mystery of the Trinity we see an ineffable and eternal love between the members of the Trinity. Jesus refers to it in His high-priestly prayer: "Father, I desire that they also, whom You have given Me, be with Me where I am, so that they may see My glory which You have given Me, for You loved Me *before the foundation of the world*" (John 17:24, italics mine).

That love must find an expression. True love always seeks ways to give. And in a demonstration of His perfect love for His Son, the Father made a pledge to the Son. And what was that pledge? He promised the Son a redeemed people—justified, sanctified, and glorified. He promised to bring the redeemed ones to glory, that they might dwell in the very place where Father and Son have dwelt since before time began, the very realm of God. And this collective body of called-out ones—a people for His name (Acts 15:14) from every tribe and people and tongue and nation (Revelation 13:7)—would form a living temple for the Holy Spirit (Ephesians 2:21–22), becoming the very dwelling-place of God.

That is the eternal promise the Father made to the Son. Why? As an expression of His love. The redeemed of humanity, then, are a gift from Father to Son.

With that in mind, consider Jesus' words in John 6:37: "All that the Father gives Me will come to Me, and the one who comes to Me I will certainly not cast out." That again affirms the utter invincibility of the Church. Every individual ever redeemed—everyone ever given the gift of faith, forgiven, and justified before God by grace—is a lovegift from the Father to the Son. And not one of them will fail or be cast out. Would Christ turn down a love-gift from His own Father?

Furthermore, the importance of the doctrine of election emerges from all this. The redeemed are chosen and given to the Son by the Father as a gift. If you are a believer, it is not because you are more clever than your unbelieving neighbors. You did not come to faith through your own ingenuity. You were drwan to Christ by God the Father (John 6:44, 65). And every individual who comes to faith is

drawn by God and given as a love-gift from the
Father to the Son, as part of a redeemed people—
the Church—promised to the Son before time began.

The full significance of God's eternal purpose
becomes clear as it is unfolded to us in the book of
Revelation. There we get a glimpse into heaven,
and what do you suppose the triumphant Church
is doing there? What occupies the glorified saints
throughout eternity? They worship and glorify the
Lamb, praising Him and serving Him, and even
reigning with Him (Revelation 22:3–5). The collective body is pictured as His bride, pure and spotless and clothed in fine linen (19:7–8). They dwell
with Him eternally where there is no night, no
tears, no sorrow, and no pain (21:4). And they glorify and serve the Lamb forever. That is the fullness
of God's purpose; that is the reason why the
Church is His gift to His Son.

Now this eternal promise involved a reciprocal
promise from the Son to the Father. Redemption
was by no means the Father's work alone. In order
to accomplish the divine plan, the Son would have
to go into the world as a member of the human
race and pay the penalty for sin. And the Son submitted completely to the Father's will. That is what
Jesus meant in John 6:38–39: "I have come down
from heaven, not to do My own will, but the will of

Him who sent Me. This is the will of Him who sent Me, that of all that He has given Me I lose nothing, but raise it up on the last day."

Redemption from sin could not be purchased by animal sacrifices or any other means. Therefore the Son came to earth for the express purpose of dying for sin. His sacrifice on the cross was an act of submission to the Father's will. Hebrews 10:4–9 makes this very point:

> For it is impossible for the blood of bulls and goats to take away sins. Therefore, when He comes into the world, He says, "Sacrifice and offering You have not desired, but a body You have prepared for Me; in whole burnt offerings and sacrifices for sin You have taken no pleasure. Then I said, 'Behold, I have come (in the scroll of the book it is written of Me) to do Your will, O God.' " After saying above, "Sacrifices and offerings and whole burnt offerings and sacrifices for sin You have not desired, nor have You taken pleasure in them" (which are offered according to the Law), then He said, "Behold, I have come to do Your will."

So the Son submitted to the Father's will, demonstrating His love for the Father. And the building of the Church is therefore not only the Father's expression of love to the Son, but also the Son's expression of love to the Father.

All of this means that the Church is something so monumental, so vast, so transcendent, that our poor minds can scarcely begin to appreciate its significance in the eternal plan of God. Our salvation as individuals is almost incidental. The real aim of God's plan is not merely to get us to heaven. But the drama of our salvation has an even grander purpose: it is an expression of eternal love within the Trinity. We're only the gift.

There's one thing more worth noting about the Father's eternal plan with regard to the Church. Romans 8:29 says that those whom the Father chose to give to the Son He also predestined to be conformed to the Son's image. Not only would He justify them, sanctify them, glorify them, and bring them to heaven so that forever and ever they could say, "Worthy is the Lamb," but He also determined that they would be made like the Son. As much as it is possible for finite humanity to resemble incarnate deity, we will be like Jesus Christ. This is "so that He would be the firstborn *[protokos]* among many brethren" (Romans 8:29). *Protokos* refers not to someone born first in chronology, but the premier one of a class. In other words, Christ is the supreme One over a whole brotherhood of people who are like Him.

Our glorification will instantly transform us into Christlikeness. John wrote, "When He appears, we will be like Him, because we will see Him just as He is" (1 John 3:2). Paul told the Galatians, "I am in labor until Christ is formed in you" (Galatians 4:19). We're being conformed to Christ's image. And the good news is that this goal will be achieved. The Church will emerge from all her trials triumphant, glorious, spotlessly arrayed to meet her Bridegroom.

How can we not rejoice in the prospect of that? How can Christians possibly be apathetic about the Church?

One exuberant new Christian stood up to give a testimony in a public meeting. He had noticed that the congregation, mostly older believers, seemed to have lost some of the joy of their salvation. He said simply, "This week I read the end of the book, and you know what? In the end, we win!" That's a pretty good eschatological perspective. The Church is ultimately invincible. The purposes of God cannot be thwarted.

There is a fascinating conclusion to all this. Paul describes it in 1 Corinthians 15:24–28:

> Then comes the end, when He hands over the kingdom to God and the Father, when He has abolished all rule and all authority and power. For He must reign until He has put all His enemies under His feet. The last enemy that will be abolished is death. For He has put all

things in subjection under His feet. But when
He says, "All things are put in subjection," it is
evident that He is excepted who put all things
in subjection to Him. When all things are
subjected to Him, then the Son Himself also
will be subjected to the One who subjected all
things to Him, so that God may be all in all.

Picture the scene. All Christ's enemies are destroyed and defeated. All things are placed in subjection to the Son. The Father has given Him the
great love-gift, the Church, to be His bride and to be
subject to Him. Christ is on the throne. All things
are now subject to Him, except the Father, who put
all things in subjection to His Son. "Then the Son
Himself also will be subjected to the One who subjected all things to Him, so that God may be all in
all" (v. 28).

In other words, when the Son brings the Church
to glory, and the Father gives it to the Son as His
eternal love-gift, then the Son will turn around and
give everything, including Himself, back to the
Father.

This is a mind-boggling look at our future. This
is God's plan for the Church. We are a people
called out for His name, redeemed, conformed to
His Son's image, made to be an immense, incom-
prehensible, all-surpassing expression of love between the persons of the Trinity. The Church is the

gift that is exchanged. This is God's eternal plan for the church. We ought to be profoundly grateful, eager, and thrilled to be a part of it.

3. The Church is the most precious reality on earth.

I love the church because it is the most precious thing on this earth, more precious than silver or gold or any other earthly commodity.

How precious is the Church? It demanded the highest price ever paid for anything. "You have been bought with a price" (1 Corinthians 6:20). What price? "You were not redeemed with perishable things like silver or gold from your futile way of life inherited by your forefathers, but with precious blood, as of a lamb unblemished and spotless, the blood of Christ" (1 Peter 1:18–19). Acts 20:28 refers to "the church of God which He purchased with His own blood."

The Church is so precious that the Son was willing to suffer the agonies of the cross and die in obedience to the Father so that this eternal love-gift could become a reality. In 2 Corinthians 8:9, the Apostle Paul reminded the Corinthians of this great reality: "You know the grace of our Lord Jesus Christ, that though He was rich, yet for your sakes He became poor, so that you through His poverty might become rich." That verse has nothing to do with earthly riches or material things. Christ was rich as God is rich, rich in glory (cf. John 17:5).

Neither is the poverty spoken of an earthly poverty. Christ divested Himself of His glory. He went from sovereign supernatural deity to taking upon Himself the form of a servant, and ultimately to a death on the cross (Colossians 2:6–8) in which all the force of divine wrath was poured out upon Him.

So the precious value of the Church is seen here in the price that was paid, when the One who was as rich as God in fullness of glory became as poor as someone alienated from God (cf. Matthew 27:46).

And, to return to the point of 2 Corinthians 8:9, Christ did this so that we might become rich. His dying made us heirs of God and joint-heirs with Christ (Romans 8:17). In other words, in giving up His heavenly riches, Christ made it possible for the Church to share in those riches. That makes the Church the most precious thing on earth.

4. *The Church is an earthly expression of heaven.*

I love the Church because it is like heaven on earth. I don't mean that the Church is perfect, or that it offers some kind of utopian escape from the realities of a sinful world. But I mean that the Church is the one place where all that occurs in heaven also occurs on earth.

Christ instructed us to pray, "Your will be done, on earth as it is in heaven" (Matthew 6:10). In what sphere is that most likely to occur? In the United States Congress? Not likely. In the Supreme Court? Probably not. In the university? No. City Hall? Don't count on it.

Where is God's will done on earth as it is in heaven? Only in one place, and that is the Church.

What goes on in heaven? If all the activities of heaven were to be brought to earth, what activities would predominate?

First of all, worship. In every biblical description where men of God had visions of heaven, the one thing that stands out most is worship. Praise, adoration, and devotion are constantly being offered to God in heaven. We see it, for example, in Isaiah 6:1–3, where the prophet Isaiah wrote,

> I saw the Lord sitting on a throne, lofty and exalted, with the train of His robe filling the temple. Seraphim stood above Him, each having six wings: with two he covered his face, and with two he covered his feet, and with two he flew. And one called out to another and said, "Holy, holy, holy, is the Lord of hosts, the whole earth is full of His glory."

We see it in Revelation 4:8–11, where John wrote,

> And the four living creatures, each one of them having six wings, are full of eyes around and within; and day and night they do not

cease to say, "Holy, holy, holy is the Lord God,
the Almighty, who was and who is and who is
to come." And when the living creatures give
glory and honor and thanks to Him who sits
on the throne, to Him who lives forever and
ever, the twenty-four elders fall down before
Him who sits on the throne, and worship Him
who lives forever and ever, and cast their
crowns before the throne, saying, "Worthy are
You, our Lord and our God, to receive glory
and honor and power; for You created all
things, and because of Your will they existed,
and were created."

In other words, every creature in heaven is per-
petually engaged in worship.

Worship is also one of the main activities of the
Church. In 1 Corinthians 14, where Paul described
what took place in a typical meeting in the early
church, he wrote, "When you assemble, each one
has a psalm, a teaching, a revelation, a tongue, an
interpretation. Let all things be done for edification"
(v. 26). There he describes activities whose design
is both to worship God and to edify the worship-
pers. And if an unbeliever came into the meeting,
this was the desired response: "the secrets of his
heart are disclosed; and so he will fall on his face
and worship God, declaring that God is certainly
among you" (v. 25).

A second activity of heaven is the exaltation of

Christ. Having finished His earthly work, Christ is now seated at the Father's right hand in glory and pure exaltation (Acts 5:31). God Himself has exalted His Son, and given Him a name above every name (Philippians 2:9). Christ is "exalted above the heavens" (Hebrews 7:26). And throughout all eternity we will be occupied exalting His name (cf. Revelation 5:11–14). Meanwhile, the Church is the one sphere on earth where Christ's name is truly and genuinely exalted.

A third activity that takes place in heaven is the preservation of purity and holiness. Heaven is a holy place. Revelation 21:8 says "the cowardly and unbelieving and abominable and murderers and immoral persons and sorcerers and idolaters and all liars" are excluded from heaven, consigned instead to the lake of fire. Revelation 22:14–15 underscores the perfect purity of heaven's inhabitants: "Blessed are those who wash their robes, so that they may have the right to the tree of life, and may enter by the gates into the city. Outside are the dogs and the sorcerers and the immoral persons and the murderers and the idolaters, and everyone who loves and practices lying." No one is admitted to heaven who is not holy (Hebrews 12:14).

Likewise, the Church on earth is charged with preserving purity within her own midst. Matthew 18:15–20 lays out a process of discipline by which the Church is to keep herself pure, if necessary through excommunication of members. It's not necessary in this context to outline the whole discipline process, but take note of the promise Christ makes in verse 18: "Truly I say to you, whatever you bind on earth shall have been bound in heaven; and whatever you loose on earth shall have been loosed in heaven."

Binding and loosing were rabbinical expressions that spoke of dealing with people's guilt. An unrepentant person was said to be bound to his sin, and a repentant person was loosed. Here Christ suggests that when a church on earth follows the proper procedure for discipline, it in effect mediates heaven's verdict in the earthly church. Heaven is in agreement with its decision. When the church on earth excommunicates an unrepentant member, the elders of that church are simply declaring what heaven has already said. Church discipline is therefore an earthly expression of heaven's holiness.

Another activity of heaven that occurs in the Church is the fellowship of the saints. Our fellowship in the church on earth is a foretaste of the perfect communion we will enjoy in heaven. The Church, then, is like an earthly expression of heaven. It is the closest we can get to heaven on earth.

There's a lot of talk these days about "user-friendly" churches. Church growth experts counsel church leaders to try to provide an atmosphere in which "unchurched" people can feel comfortable and at home. That strikes me as an utterly wrong-headed approach to the church. Unchurched people who come into our fellowship ought to leave saying to themselves, "I have never seen anything like this on earth!" If they walk away thinking, *Ah, that felt comfortable; that was familiar*—then something is seriously wrong! The church should be like a preview of heaven.

The Apostle Paul wrote of "the household of God, which is the church of the living God, the pillar and support of the truth" (1 Timothy 3:15). More than any other institution on earth, the Church is where the truth of God is uphelp. The Church is called to lift up the truth and hold it high. Employing the truth as a weapon, we are to smash the ideological fortresses of Satan's lies (2 Corinthians 10:3–5). And it is in the pursuit of that goal that the Church will ultimately realize her greatest triumph.

All of that is why I love the Church. And as long as the Lord gives me breath, I hope to invest my life and energies in the ministry and advancement of the church's mission.

Glorious things of thee are spoken,
Zion, city of our God;
He whose word cannot be broken
Formed thee for His own abode.
On the Rock of Ages founded,
What can shake thy sure repose?
With salvation's walls surrounded,
Thou mayst smile at all thy foes.

John Newton

Glorious Things of Thee are Spoken

Joel R. Beeke on the Doctrine of the Church

How important is the church in the life of the individual Christian? This question has been answered in various ways. At one end of the spectrum is the clericalism and absolutism of Roman Catholicism, in which the visible and institutional church, administered by a hierarchy of priests, bishops, and pope, claims and wields total power over the believer in matters pertaining to this life and the next. At the other end is modern American evangelicalism with its intense subjectivism and individualism, which makes Christianity consist only in personal faith, and suspiciously regards the church as "organized religion." Many agree with the notion that the church is a voluntary society.[1] "You don't have to attend church to be a Christian," they say. As a result, the church commands scant regard for her ordinances and even less loyalty from her adherents. As an institution, the church must compete for support with the whole welter of

---

[1] Michael Horton, *We Believe: Recovering the Essentials of the Apostles' Creed* (Nashville, Tenn.: Word, 1998), p. 193.

Christian crusades, mission agencies, schools, publications, broadcasts, charities, and fund drives that
crowd the landscape of evangelical America.

Both extremes are rooted in unbiblical views of
the church. Both are unacceptable to the mind of
the Reformation. While breaking with the clericalism and absolutism of Rome, the Reformers
nonetheless maintained a high view of the church.
John Calvin wrote, "If we do not prefer the church
to all other objects of our interest, we are unworthy
of being counted among her members." Calvin
agreed with Augustine who said, "He cannot have
God for his Father who refuses to have the church
for his mother." To this Calvin added, "For there is
no other way to enter into life unless this mother
conceive us in her womb, give us birth, nourish us
at her breast, and lastly, unless she keep us under
her care and guidance until, putting off mortal
flesh, we become like the angels."[2]

In the past, Reformed believers have profoundly
cherished the church. Today, that sense of appreciation is waning in general. Many Protestants have
depreciated the place the church occupies as
Christ's institution.[3] This lowered view of the

---

[2] *Institutes of the Christian Religion*, ed. John T. McNeill, trans.
Ford Lewis Battles (Philadelphia: Westminster Press, 1960),
4.1.1, 4.1.4.

[3] John Murray, "The Church—Its Identity, Functions, and

church is fostered by a lack of understanding about what the church truly is as Christ's institution. It disregards Jesus' words to Peter, "Upon this rock I will build My church" (Matthew 16:18). We can't really understand what the church is and why we should appreciate it until we truly understand the meaning of those words. To that end, I'll address the status of the church as belonging to Christ ("My church"), the substance of the church as founded upon Christ ("upon this rock"), and the success of the church as the workmanship of Christ ("I will build")—all of which should increasingly prompt us to cherish the church.

The Church's Status: Belonging to Christ

When Jesus tells Peter, "I will build My church," He declares that the church belongs to Him. The word "My" in the original is moved from its normal grammatical position to show that emphasis. Jesus did not use that possessive pronoun lightly. Significantly, He talked about "My Father," "My friends," "My teaching," and "My church," but never about "My money" or "My property."

Jesus used the Greek word *ekklesia* to describe His church.[4] The only other place in the gospels

---

Resources," in *Collected Writings of John Murray* (Edinburgh: Banner of Truth Trust, 1976), 1:238.

[4] Lothar Coenen, "Church," in *The New Theological Dictio-*

where *ekklesia* is used is Matthew 18:17. But the term is used seventy times in the Septuagint (the Greek translation of the Old Testament) as the translation of the Hebrew term *qahal*, which describes the congregation or assembly of God's chosen and privileged people, Israel. As God's *ekklesia*, Israel is called to know, love, and serve Him.

John Murray wrote, "When Jesus speaks of 'My church,' He is thinking of those gathered and knit together after the pattern provided by the Old Testament as the people for His possession, as the community which He is to constitute, and which stands in a relation to Him comparable to the congregation of the Lord in the Old Testament."[5] Several aspects of God's relationship with the *ekklesia* are still true of the church today. Both Israel and the church are called by sovereign grace out of Egypt (Hosea 11:1–5) and the world. Both are called by God into a covenantal relationship with Him to accomplish a vital kingdom task. Both

---

nary of New Testament Theology, ed. Colin Brown (Grand Rapids, Mich.: Zondervan, 1975), 1:291–307; D. Douglas Bannerman, *The Scripture Doctrine of the Church* (1887; rpt. Grand Rapids, Mich.: Eerdmans, 1955), pp. 571–76; Thomas Lindsay, *The Church and the Ministry in the Early Centuries* (London: Hodder and Stoughton, 1907), pp. 4–5, 10–11.

5 "The Nature and Unity of the Church," in *Collected Writings of John Murray,* 2:323.

are called to worship God in community. And both are called to future inheritance in the heavenly Canaan.[6]

The New Testament uses the term *ekklesia* in five distinct ways:

• The elect church, or the entire body of believers in heaven (the church triumphant) and on earth (the church militant) who are or shall be spiritually united to Christ.

• The worldwide church, or everyone in the world who professes faith in Christ and worships Him under the guidance of appointed office-bearers.

• The local church, or believers of a specific congregation who worship God together.

• A group of congregations who affiliate with each other under a common government.

• Church office-bearers, or appointed leaders who represent a local church.[7]

When Jesus said "My church" in Matthew 16, He was claiming God's people as His own. The *ekklesia* is thus His assembly, His people, bound to Him with ties far deeper than those of family or friendship. The *ekklesia* is defined in Matthew 16:18

---

6 David Watson, *I Believe in the Church* (London: Hodder and Stoughton, 1978), pp. 67–74.

7 James Bannerman, *The Church of Christ* (1869; London: Banner of Truth Trust, 1960), 1:6–15.

by her saving relationship to Jesus the Messiah, who has done for her what the old sacrificial system merely foreshadowed in its attempt to atone for sin. The *ekklesia* is a people bonded to Christ in love, mercy, forgiveness, and dependence.[8]

Christ's assembly started with a small group of ordinary people. But Jesus looked at His disciples and spoke about His church. "You are Mine, you belong to Me," He said. We value what belongs to famous people. If I were to ask you how much you would give me for an antique pen, you might offer me $20 to $50. But if I were to say, "This is the pen that John Calvin used to write the *Institutes of the Christian Religion*," you would probably offer me considerably more. The value of the object would increase substantially because of the person who owned it.

The church belongs to Jesus Christ. It does not belong to us. It is precious because the Son of God said, "This is My church," and even more so because of what Christ did to make it His. In Ephesians 5:25, Paul says that Christ "loved the church, and gave Himself for it." In Acts 20:28, Paul speaks of "the church of God" which Christ "hath purchased with His own blood."

Golgotha, where Christ died for His church, was

---

8 Cyril Charles Richardson, *The Church through the Centuries* (London: Religious Book Club, 1938), pp. 19–23.

not a pretty place. It was not a sentimental spot for tourists, but a place of blood and death and punishment. Yet this bloody punishment of sin is precisely what we deserve, for the wages of sin are death and hell (Romans 6:23; Revelation 21:8), where the smoke of torment justly ascends day and night forever (Revelation 14:10–11). Only when we see how ugly sin is, and how justly we deserve such punishment, do we perceive the wonder of what transpired at Golgotha.

To begin to appreciate what Christ did on Golgotha for His Church, we must know how God views sin. God condemns original sin and actual sin, sinful deeds and sinful words, sinful thoughts and sinful attitudes, sin in its branches and sin in its root. God hates sin, outlaws sin, and judges sin. The God who is light, and in whom is no darkness at all, indicts and condemns sin as a contradiction of His nature. John Bunyan put it well: "Sin is the daring of God's justice, the jeering of His patience, the slighting of His power, the contempt of His love." God will thereupon punish sin with the endless death of the soul in hell. In a word, *hell* is what God thinks of sin.

Reformed evangelicals are often criticized for being preoccupied with sin. Yet the most appalling utterances about sin are found in Scripture, not in our confessions of faith or in the words of Calvin or

Bunyan. What is human society really like? The prophet Isaiah said Israel as a society was like a man covered in boils and ulcers from the crown of his head to the soles of his feet (Isaiah 1:6). Jesus said that "out of the heart proceed evil thoughts, murders, adulteries, fornications, thefts, false witness, blasphemies" (Matthew 15:19). Paul likened human society to a community of snakes with poison under its lips (Romans 3:13). The book of Revelation compares the condition of man to a bottomless pit opened by a great divine hand, with the smoke of depravity and the everlasting burnings of hell pouring forth and obscuring the light of the sun.

Lest you think such biblical illustrations go too far in describing the depravity of man, consider what western civilization has done. What kind of depravity was exhibited when Africans were enslaved and whipped into submission? What about those who subjected Jews to gas chambers, incinerators, and torture? What about those who vacuum unborn children out of wombs, cut them up, incinerate them, and then boast of "the right to choose"? We stand before God in a corporate silence of guilt.

Society's history is no different from our own as individuals. The records of each of us testify against us. Our thoughts, fantasies, emotions, resentments, bitterness, and self-pity condemn us.

Our words, which are so often harsh, cruel, and cold, condemn us. And our actions are little better: what we do even to our dearest friends and those who most depend upon us condemns us.

So immense is our depravity before God that there is only one way in which we can be reconciled to Him. That way is through God's Son, who came into this world to take on our flesh and dwell among us. The eternal Son of God born in a stable to dwell among men! The immortal Son clothing Himself with rags of mortality! God, who made man after His image, Himself made in man's image! And if that wasn't enough, He also offered that life as a ransom for needy sinners like us. "I must die," He said to His disciples from the beginning. "The bridegroom will be wrenched away from you and you will fast in that day. But I must go to Jerusalem for your welfare, to be a ransom for your sin. I did not come to be ministered to but to minister" (cf. Matthew 20:28; Philippians 2:6–8).

The only way God can forgive our sin is through Christ. Jesus endured the wrath of a sin-hating God against us, tasting death for us, entering the lake of fire for us, going into the bottomless pit as our substitute. "He descended into hell" and "gave up the ghost." That was what Golgotha was all about. When you sing about the wondrous cross upon which your Savior died, you should not think of something pleasant and beautiful and refreshing, but rather of everything that is ugly and atrocious and revolting. Golgotha was a place of skulls and bones and bleeding flesh.

Three crude crosses, dingy and blood-stained, support three naked bodies in that awful place. Every insult possible is shouted against one of those prisoners, the one in the center, whose name is Jesus. Soldiers, spectators, priests, and elders hurl their hate against Jesus. The only one who dares to speak in His defense is a dying thief. The tender-hearted women who followed Him are silent; the disciples who loved Him are too terrified to rise in His defense. His brothers and His friends have forsaken Him. Worst of all, so has God. The face of the Father that Jesus always turned to in love and adoration is now turned away. He has become an outcast from His Father's house.

This is what God thinks about sin and depravity. Sin is terrifying in the presence of Sinai's thunder and lightning, but sin is most bitter, as Thomas Watson said, in the "red glass" of Christ's suffering. Jesus was separated from all that is good and lovely, abandoned to the cruel hands of the most merciless men on the planet. Even God, who had been with His Son to support and encourage Him throughout His ministry, was absent in that hour in any favorable sense. There Christ hangs in the naked flame of God's holiness bearing our sin, wounded for our transgressions. The unclean place, the passions of the mob, the sufferings of the soul, the darkened sun, the coldness of God and His holy revulsion against sin—such are the wages of sin!

This is the dowry that Jesus Christ paid to His Father for His bride, the Church. We must remember that incalculable dowry of suffering and blood when we are tempted to slight the Church, take her for granted, or neglect our duties toward her. If the Lord Jesus Christ cherished the Church so much that He died for her, is it too much for Him to ask His followers to cherish the Church and live for her?

Cherishing the Church as the purchased bride of Christ doesn't negate all criticism of the Church. But healthy criticism, which is based on Scripture, is measured out with sorrow and pain. Unhealthy criticism is sour and destructive, and is based on human feelings. Men who love their wives can take a great deal of criticism against themselves, but they do not take kindly to unkind comments directed against their spouses. Similarly, Jesus Christ does not approve when we thoughtlessly criticize His bride (cf. Ephesians 5:22–33).

The Church's Substance: Founded upon Christ

Jesus said, "Upon this rock I will build My church." Wars have been fought over the meaning of those words, people have shed blood and spilled ink over them, and church leaders and synods have argued over them. Those very words are also inscribed in letters of gold on the great dome of St. Peter's in Rome. In fact, Roman Catholicism says that the rock is Peter, who served as Christ's vicar on earth. Peter, in turn, is claimed as founder of the church of Rome. His role as "vicar of Christ" was passed to succeeding bishops, Rome claims.

Most Protestants acknowledge that these words refer partly to Peter, whose name derives from the word for "stone."[9] But the rock Christ speaks of refers less to Peter's person than it does to his confession: "Thou art the Christ, the Son of the living God" (Matthew 16:16). Peter here is spokesman for

---

[9] This acknowledgment is not a capitulation to Rome's view. Even if the rock were referring wholly to Peter, the Roman Catholic would still have to prove several things that are not supported by the text. John A. Broadus said that these include: that Peter alone was to be the founder of Christianity, that he was vice-regent of God and the sovereign of all Christians, that his supposed authority was transmissible as well as actually transmitted to the leading official of the church at Rome, and that Peter lived and died at Rome (*Commentary on the Gospel of Matthew* [1886; rpt. Valley Forge, Pa.: Judson Press, n.d.], pp. 356–57).

the rest of the disciples, whose confession matches his. That is evident from Jesus' question: "Whom say ye that I am?" (Matthew 16:15). And that explains why in Matthew 18:18 the rest of the disciples receive the same keys of the kingdom that were previously given to Peter (Matthew 16:19). If the rock were Peter, Christ would probably have said, "You are Peter (*petra,* rock) and upon this Peter (*petra,* rock) I will build My church." Instead, Christ used a diversity of form and gender in Greek words (*petros* and *petra*) which is "too abrupt and marked to be unmeaning and fortuitous," wrote Joseph Addison Alexander.[10] The rock was not Peter, an erring, unstable man, but the mighty truth the Father had revealed to Peter, namely, the Messiahship and divine Sonship of Jesus. Though Peter himself cannot be entirely separated from his confession, the focus in this context is on his confession of Christ's true identity.

When Christ therefore declares, "Upon this rock I will build My church," He refers to what Peter has confessed—His own identity and office as the Son of God and Israel's promised Messiah.[11] The Church shows on what she is built by her confes-

---

[10] *The Gospel According to Matthew* (London: James Nisbet, 1861), p. 439.

[11] R. B. Kuiper, *The Glorious Body of Christ* (London: Banner of Truth Trust, 1966), pp. 67–68.

sion. She rests on the reality of the objective revelation which Peter confessed. That is the Church's
true foundation; the true Church is built upon it.
"The truth that Jesus Christ is the promised
Messiah, very God and very Man in one Person, the
anointed Savior of the world, is the main ground-
stone whereupon the faith of all believers is
founded, as upon a rock," wrote David Dickson.[12]

Thus, the rock on which the Church is built is
Jesus Christ, the Son of the living God. This does
justice to the classical distinction Jesus maintained
between *petros* (stone) and *petra* (rock), which may
indicate, according to Alexander, that "while Peter
was a stone, i.e., a fragment of the rock, his Master
was the rock itself."[13] Christ alone is the chief
cornerstone of the structure (1 Corinthians 3:11;
Ephesians 2:20; 1 Peter 2:4–6). As the Dutch annotations summarize, "*Rock;* namely, on this thy confession which thou makest of Me, or on Me, whom
thou hast confessed. For Christ alone is the foundation of His Church (1 Corinthians 3:11)."[14]

Whatever else we may say about these words,

---

[12] *Matthew* (1647; rpt. Edinburgh: Banner of Truth Trust,
1981), p. 224.

[13] Alexander, *Matthew,* p. 439.

[14] *The Dutch Annotations upon the whole Bible,* trans.
Theodore Haak (London: Henry Hills, 1657), vol. 2, on
Matthew 16:18.

we can certainly say that the Church is founded upon Jesus Christ and that the chief article of the Christian faith is trust in Christ. That's the basic mark of belonging to what the Reformers, following Augustine and John Wycliffe, called "the invisible church." Calvin said that the invisible church consisted of the elect, whose names are in the Lamb's Book of Life (Revelation 21:27), and who will become known by saving faith and its fruits (Matthew 7:20).[15] Thus a person can be a member of the visible church (the church as we see it) of professing believers, yet not be a part of the invisible church (the church as God sees it) of genuine believers who have a true saving relationship with

---

[15] John Wycliffe, *Tractatus de Ecclesia,* ed. Johann Loserth (London: Treubner, 1886), p. 2; Calvin, *Institutes,* 4.1.7; David N. Wiley, "The Church as the Elect in the Theology of Calvin," in *John Calvin and the Church: A Prism of Reform,* ed. Timothy George (Louisville: Westminster/John Knox Press, 1990), pp. 96–117. Cf. Geddes MacGregor, *Corpus Christi: The Nature of the Church According to the Reformed Tradition* (Philadelphia: Westminster Press, 1958); George H. Tavard, *Holy Writ or Holy Church: The Crisis of the Protestant Reformation* (New York: Harper & Brothers, 1959); Kilian McDonnell, *John Calvin, the Church, and the Eucharist* (Princeton, N. J.: Princeton University Press, 1967); Paul D. L. Avis, *The Church in the Theology of the Reformers* (London: Marshall Morgan & Scott, 1981); Harro P. Höpfl, *The Christian Polity of John Calvin* (Cambridge, England: Cambridge University Press, 1982).

Christil.[16] The invisible church is the true church,
said Heinrich Bullinger, a great Swiss Reformer.[17]

That distinction guards us against equating
membership in the visible church with salvation.
Just belonging to a church doesn't make someone
a true believer any more than owning an organ
makes one a true musician. The saving work of the
Holy Spirit welds Christians together. Whatever
their differences, all true Christians are saved by
Spirit-worked faith and trust in Christ alone (*solus
Christus*). A church so constituted builds on Christ
as on a rock.

Jesus Christ is the Mediator, Minister, and
Surety of His Church. But the substance with

---

[16] Bannerman, *The Church of Christ*, 1:29–40. Many in the
Reformed community in recent decades have voiced concern
about the formula and doctrine of the invisible church, in-
cluding John Murray (*Collected Writings*, 1:231–36), though
Murray later muted that criticism (ibid., 4:262). Cf. Kuiper,
The Glorious Body of Christ, pp. 26–30; Watson, *I Believe in
The Church*, pp. 332–33; Peter Toon, *God's Church for Today*
(Westchester, Ill.: Crossway, 1980), pp. 26–28; Jelle Faber,
"The Doctrine of the Church in Reformed Confessions,"
Essays in Reformed Doctrine (Neerlandia, Alberta: Inheritance,
1990), pp. 112–15; Stuart R. Jones, "The Invisible Church of
the Westminster Confession of Faith," *Westminster Theological
Journal* 59 (1997):71–85.

[17] *The Decades of Henry Bullinger*, ed. Thomas Harding, trans.
H. I. (Cambridge, England: University Press, 1852), 5:7–9.

which He builds His Church is sinners. Jesus
changes sinners by His power, makes them confes-
sors of His name, and works commitment in their
lives. When this is forgotten, the church weakens
and begins to die. It is a scandal when churches
list dozens, sometimes hundreds of families on
their rolls of membership who seldom attend worship services and show that they have no personal
faith in Christ, no living relationship with Him.
Many churches today are strong in membership but
weak in discipleship. Such churches may seem
strong numerically, but they are built on sand and
will soon break down under stress. "The church is
most evangelistic when she is least concerned
about impressing the world or with adding to her
numbers," Iain Murray says.

An inactive church member is a contradiction in
terms. If we do not cherish the Church and view
membership as a great privilege, we need to question if we are truly a part of the Church. We cannot
expect to meet with the church triumphant in glory
if we neglect to meet with the church militant on
earth. Freelance or non-participatory Christianity
negates the entire concept of a New Testament
church as a corporate witness of redeemed fellowship.

Implied in the rock of Peter's confession in
Jesus Christ are the historic attributes of the

Church, best summarized by the Nicene Creed's confession of "one holy, catholic, and apostolic church."[18] Roman Catholics and Protestants have always taught that those attributes are inseparable from the essence of the Church. But while Roman Catholics emphasize the visible, institutional form of those attributes, Protestants focus on their Spirit-worked and experiential character. As Charles Hodge said, "If the church is the body of those who are united to Christ by the indwelling of the Holy Spirit, then the indwelling of the Spirit must make the Church holy, visible, perpetual, one, catholic."[19] We need to understand how each attribute begins with and finds fulfillment in Jesus Christ, the Church's rock and foundation, in order to appreciate and practice them.

---

[18] G. C. Berkouwer, *The Church*, trans. James E. Davison (Grand Rapids: Eerdmans, 1976), is entirely devoted to the unity, catholicity, apostolicity, and holiness of the church as she expounds her true ministry. Cf. standard works of systematic theology and works on the Belgic Confession of Faith (Articles 27–29), the Heidelberg Catechism (Q. 54), the Westminster Confession (Chapter 25), and the Larger Catechism (Q. 61–64) (Joel R. Beeke and Sinclair B. Ferguson, *Reformed Confessions Harmonized* [Grand Rapids, Mich.: Baker, 1999], pp. 188–93).

[19] Charles Hodge, *Discussions in Church Polity* (New York: Charles Scribner's Sons, 1878), p. 8.

Practicing the Unity of the Church

The Nicene Creed confesses "one church" (*unam ecclesiam*), meaning that the Church is built upon one rock, one Messiah, one confession. The Westminster Confession adds that the Church's unity lies in Jesus Christ: "The catholic or universal church, which is invisible, consists of the whole number of the elect, that have been, are, or shall be gathered into one, under Christ the Head thereof; and is the spouse, the body, the fullness of Him that filleth all in all" (Chapter 25:1). That the Church is Christ's body, and He the Head (Colossians 1:18), implies that Christ and the Church are complementary, for a body and a head cannot exist without each other.

Wilhelmus à Brakel stressed that same idea by saying the Church and Christ are each other's property. Their union is affirmed by the gift of Christ to the Church, Christ's purchase of and victory for the Church, the indwelling of Christ's Spirit within the Church, and the Church's surrender by faith and love to Christ.[20] To think of Christ without the Church is to sever what God has wedded together in holy union.

The Church is organically related to Christ more

---

[20] Wilhelmus à Brakel, *The Christian's Reasonable Service,* ed. Joel R. Beeke, trans. Bartel Elshout (Ligonier, Pa.: Soli Deo Gloria, 1993), 2:87–90.

profoundly than any organic relationship that falls within the realm of our experience; she is rooted and built up in Christ (Colossians 2:7), she is clothed with Christ (Romans 13:14), and she cannot live without Christ (Philippians 1:21). "The church is in Christ as Eve was in Adam," wrote Richard Hooker.

The Church is Christ's fullness because the plenitude of His grace is poured out upon her (John 1:16; Colossians 2:9–10). The Church, Christ's mystical body, "is like a vessel into which the fullness of Christ is poured," wrote L. S. Thornton. "He fills it with Himself."[21] Christ's attributes—truth, power, mercy, love, patience, goodness, righteousness, wisdom—are both the embodiment of the Church's virtue and her resources.

All the members of Christ's body are likewise united to one another because of their common Head (1 Corinthians 12). All true believers who confess Christ as their exclusive Savior are "joined and united with heart and will, by the power of faith, in one and the same Spirit," says the Belgic Confession in Article 27. They are united as members of the household of God, the community of Christ, and the fellowship of the Spirit. There is one gospel (Acts 4:12), one revelation (1 Corinthi-

---

[21] *The Common Life in the Body of Christ* (London: Dacre Press, 1950), p. 310.

ans 2:6–10), one baptism (Ephesians 4:5), and one Lord's Supper (1 Corinthians 10:17).

A. A. Hodge said that if there is one God, one Christ, one Spirit, and one cross, there can only be one Church.[22] The believers of this one Church are described in New Testament images such as salt of the earth, the holy temple, the new creation, sanctified slaves, sons of God, and fighters against Satan.[23] They are many branches in one vine, many sheep in one flock, and many stones in one building. The Church is "a chosen generation, a royal priesthood, a holy nation, a peculiar people; that ye should show forth the praises of Him who hath called you out of darkness into His marvelous light" (1 Peter 2:9).

The Church's oneness in Christ is indestructible, for it comes from Him. Her unity can be disrupted, however. And when it is, we should feel shame and grief at how divided the Church can become because of her unfaithfulness to Christ and her declension from the apostolic pattern of unity. Sins such as inattention to doctrinal and practical

---

22 *Confession of Faith* (1869; London: Banner of Truth Trust, 1958), pp. 310ff.

23 Paul Minear lists 96 figures and analogies that are applied to the church in the New Testament (*Images of the New Testament* [Philadelphia: Westminster Press, 1960], pp. 268–69).

purity (1 Timothy 6:11–21), autonomy (1 Corinthians 1:10–17), factionalism (1 Corinthians 3:1–23), lust for power (3 John 9), unwillingness to seek reconciliation (Matthew 5:23–26), failure to maintain church discipline (Matthew 18:15–20), and unwillingness to help needy believers (Matthew 25:31–46) tear apart the body of Christ, causing church and denominational splits.[24] Of the 23,000-plus church denominations today, more than 700 are Reformed.[25]

Still, even the multiplicity of church denominations caused by rifts between believers cannot divide the true family of Christ. Brothers and sisters in a family may quarrel and separate, but they still remain members of one family. Likewise, the Church is one body in Christ with many members (Romans 12:3–8; 1 Corinthians 12:27), one family of God the Father (Ephesians 4:6), and one fellowship in the Spirit (Acts 4:32; Ephesians 4:31–32). As Paul wrote to the Ephesians, "There is one body, and one Spirit, even as ye are called in one hope of

---

[24] John M. Frame, *Evangelical Reunion: Denominations and the Body of Christ* (Grand Rapids, Mich.: Baker, 1991), p. 28.

[25] Cf. *World Christian Encyclopedia* (1997); Jean-Jacques Bauswein and Lukas Vischer, eds., *The Reformed Family Worldwide: A Survey of Reformed Churches, Theological Schools and International Organizations* (Grand Rapids, Mich.: Eerdmans, 1998).

your calling; one Lord, one faith, one baptism, one God and Father of all, who is above all, and through all, and in you all" (4:4–6).

Rightly understood, the church's oneness should help us avoid the kind of unity that a church claims at the expense of her confessions of truth. Some divisions are essential to keep the true church separate from the false. "Division is better than agreement in evil," George Hutcheson said. Those who support spurious unity by tolerating error and heresy forget that a split based on biblical essentials helps to preserve the true unity of the body of Christ.

An organization that moves away from faithful teaching, true worship, and obedient discipling ceases to be a church. As John Calvin said, "Those who wish to build the church by rejecting the doctrine of the Word build a pigsty, and not the church of God." John Brown added, "The suffering of gross error in the church must be very sinful. It brings contempt on the oracles and ordinances of God, [and] gives Satan opportunity to employ ordinances and ministers as instruments of rebellion against God."[26]

The church's oneness should help us avoid the

---

[26] *Practical Piety Exemplified and Illustrated in Casuistical Hints* (Glasgow: Bruce, 1783), p. 330.

kind of denominationalism[27] produced by splits over nonessential doctrines as well as egotistical differences. Such splits violate the unity of the body of Christ. As Samuel Rutherford warned, "It is a fearful sin to make a rent and a hole in Christ's mystical body because there is a spot in it."[28] Such disunity offends the Father who longs to see His family living in harmony; it offends the Son who died to break down walls of hostility; and it offends the Spirit who dwells within believers to help them live in unity.

Church members must realize that they cannot touch any part of the Church's body without affecting the whole body (1 Corinthians 12). Disunity affects the whole Church, including its work of evangelism. In John 17, Jesus prayed for the unity of the Church so the world would believe that God sent His Son to be Savior of the world. Authentic Church unity, which is a startling contrast to the strife of the world, is a sign to the world of the unity that exists between the Father and the Son.

---

[27] On the disadvantages of denominationalism, see John Murray, *Collected Writings*, 1:270–71, 275–76, and Frame, *Evangelical Reunion*, pp. 45–56.

[28] Cf. Bullinger, *Decades*, 5:49–92; Thomas M'Crie, *The Unity of the Church* (1821; reprint Dallas: Presbyterian Heritage, 1989); David L. Smith, *All God's People: A Theology of the Church* (Wheaton, Ill.: Victor, 1996), 393–407.

Christians therefore should work for unity in the Church. As John Murray wrote, "If we are once convinced of the evil of schism in the body of Christ, we shall then be constrained to preach the evil, to bring conviction to the hearts of others also, to implore God's grace and wisdom in remedying the evil, and to devise ways and means of healing these ruptures."[29] We need to follow Matthew Henry's advice: "In the great things of religion be of a mind, but when there is not a unity of sentiment, let there be a union of affections."

Authentic Church unity is not promoted by exclusive denominationalism, nor by the kind of ecumenism that embraces everyone, even those who deny apostolic doctrine. Rather, authentic unity is based on the work of the Spirit, who binds the Church together and purifies it as Christ's bride.[30] The Spirit dwells within believers and endows them with the gifts to practice unity. That unity is a strong and attractive testimony of the gospel of Christ. Consequently, Paul urged the Corinthians, Ephesians, and Philippians to be of one mind in the Spirit and to be joined and knit together so that they might grow up in every way in Christ

---

[29] *Collected Writings,* 2:335. Cf. Kuiper, *Glorious Body of Christ,* pp. 46–55.

[30] Edmund P. Clowney, *The Doctrine of the Church* (Philadelphia: Presbyterian and Reformed, 1976), p. 59.

(1 Corinthians 3:1–17; Philippians 1:27; Ephesians 4:1–16). Unity is not something to be created by Christians, but something to be safeguarded by the Church of all ages through the work of the Spirit.

Despite false attempts at unity and fractionalistic denominationalism, true believers will continue to be united as members of one body of Christ until the end of time, when every external division will disappear. There will be no denominations in heaven. There Christ's prayer that all believers may be one will find true fulfillment (John 17:20–26). In heaven, the unity of the body of Christ will be resplendent (Revelation 7:9-17). What we now can hardly believe by faith will then be gloriously evident by sight.

Practicing the Holiness of the Church

The Belgic Confession of Faith describes the Church as a "holy congregation of true Christian believers, all expecting their salvation in Jesus Christ, being washed in His blood and sanctified and sealed by the Holy Spirit." This is based on the New Testament's three-part description of the Church's holiness:

1. The Church is holy in *principle*. Each believer is a member of Christ through Christ's substitutionary death and righteousness (2 Corinthians 5:21; Hebrews 12:10–11). Because Christ is the Son

of the living God, His holiness is imputed to the
invisible church so that, as the Heidelberg Catechism says, from God's perspective in Christ, it is
as if she "never had had nor committed any sin"
(Q. 60). In Christ, all believers, individually and as
members of the corporate Church, are declared
holy.

2. The Church is holy in *practice*. The bond of
union between Christ and the Church is the Spirit,
who dwells in both. The Church is directed by the
Spirit according to the Word, and her sanctification is dependent upon the Spirit's indwelling. By
the Spirit, the Church is ethically holy in Christ
(1 Corinthians 6:14–7:10). No wonder, then, that
the New Testament stresses inward rather than
ritual holiness. Basic to this is the witness of Jesus
Himself, who as the Son of man lived perfectly
holy, for He "did no sin; neither was guile found in
His mouth" (1 Peter 2:22).

Christ is the Church's rock in sanctity. In His
incarnation, Christ sanctified Himself for His
Church so that through Him we might be sanctified before the Father. What the Church is in
Christ—holy—she must increasingly become
through the Holy Spirit. Her status is perfectly holy
in Christ, but her daily condition must become increasingly holy by the Spirit of Christ. Sanctification is a lifelong process of conforming the believer

to the character of God the Father, to the image of Christ, and to the mind of the Spirit.

3. The Church's holiness is in *process*. The New Testament envisages holiness as the progressive transformation of the entire person of believers. 1 Thessalonians 5:23: "The very God of peace sanctify you wholly; and I pray God your whole spirit and soul and body be preserved blameless unto the coming of our Lord Jesus Christ." The word "holy" means to be set apart. As Israel of the Old Testament was set apart from people who did not worship God (Exodus 19:6), so the Church of the New Testament is commanded to be set apart from the world (Hebrews 12:22–25). As members of Christ's Church, we are called to separate from all unbelief, and to consecrate ourselves to God and to serve Him in every sphere of life. Holiness must be cultivated in privacy with God, in the confidentiality of our homes, in the competitiveness of our occupation, in the pleasures of social friendship, in relation with our unevangelized neighbors and the world's hungry and unemployed, as well as in Sunday worship. Paul said in 1 Timothy 4:4–5 that everything is to be sanctified.

The New Testament emphasizes that the pursuit of comprehensive holiness is to be expected of all true followers of Christ. A common term for all believers is holy ones (*hagioi*), usually translated "saints." *Hagioi* describes ordinary believers who are pure and free from guilt or moral pollution through Christ.[31] That doesn't mean members of the Church are sinless, however. Paul knew very well that the Corinthians, Ephesians, and Philippians, whom he greeted as saints, were not perfect. Neither was the apostle himself, who confessed, "Not as though I had already attained, either were already perfect: but I follow after, if that I may apprehend that for which also I am apprehended of Christ Jesus" (Philippians 3:12).

The Church is full of spots, wrinkles, and defects. She is delivered from the dominion of sin, but not from sin itself. She no longer clings to sin, but sin clings to her. Perfect holiness is beyond her reach in this life, but it nevertheless remains her goal. She pursues and seeks to "perfect holiness in the fear of God" (2 Corinthians 7:1). The Church's holiness, though real and attainable because of Christ's work in her midst by His Word and Spirit, is only inceptive and progressive in this life. But the Church anticipates complete, eschatological holiness, when she will be fully translated into the presence of her holy Savior. Then she will reign with Christ as the Church triumphant.

---

[31] Hodge, *Discussions in Church Polity,* p. 6.

Practicing the Catholicity of the Church

The term "catholic" derives from the Greek word *katholikos,* which is a combination of the pronoun *kata* and the adjective *holos. Kata* means "throughout," and *holos* means "whole." Thus, catholic means "throughout the whole," or "that which is common to the whole." Hippocrates, the father of medical science, used the word "catholic" to describe a disease that made the whole body suffer.

Philodemon enlarged the meaning of the term when he wrote about "catholic traditions." Polybios used the term "catholic history." Ignatius of Antioch was the first to apply the word to the church.[32] "Where Jesus Christ is, there is the catholic church," he wrote in 110 A.D.[33] So *katholikos* came to mean perfect, complete, and all-encompassing as well as general or whole. All of that is implied in the Belgic Confession's statement: "We believe and profess one catholic, or universal, church."[34]

When our forefathers spoke of the catholicity or universality of the church, they referred to three things:

---

[32]Faber, *Essays in Reformed Doctrine,* p. 74.

[33] *Smyrn.* 8.2, cited by C. C. Richardson, ed., *Early Christian Fathers* (Philadelphia: Westminster Press, 1953), p. 115.

[34] For the catholicity of the Belgic Confession, see Faber, *Essays in Reformed Doctrine,* pp. 79–85.

1. The worldwide, universal character of the New Testament Church. The Old Testament Church was largely restricted to the nation of Israel, whereas the New Testament Church is international in scope. Jesus declared His catholic mission to the Gentiles: "Other sheep I have, which are not of this fold: them also I must bring, and they shall hear My voice; and there shall be one fold, and one shepherd" (John 10:16). He commanded His disciples: "Go ye into all the world, and preach the gospel to every creature" (Mark 16:15).

The Church transcended its national boundaries on Pentecost—"Whosoever shall call on the name of the Lord shall be saved," Peter said (Acts 2:21)—and has been catholic ever since. It now transcends all racial, ethnic, or gender differences (Galatians 3:27–28) to join people of every tribe and nation into one fellowship. The one, holy, catholic Church is united in Christ into one faith, lordship, and end. The list of nations in Acts 2 is a prelude to the multitude of peoples, nations, and tongues that will sing the new song of the Lamb together in glory forever (Revelation 5:9).

2. The continuity of the Church. The Church is universal not only geographically, but also chronologically. Believers who presently participate in the fellowship of God's people are members of the

community of God's people who have gone before them as well as believers who will one day follow them. They anticipate worshipping Christ in the great assembly with all the saints of every age (Revelation 7:9).

Because Jesus Christ is the same yesterday, today, and forever, the Church has a glorious past, present, and future. The Church of the past is triumphant now in heaven. The Church of the present is fighting the holy war of faith on earth. The Church of the future is already chosen to be born and saved.

3. The spaciousness of its offer of salvation through Christ. The gospel is catholic in its offer of grace. "Him that cometh to Me I will in no wise cast out," Christ promised (John 6:37). That invitation is the rock of the Church's catholicity. Believers must promote this catholicity by evangelizing people of all nations (Matthew 28:19–20), and by helping believers around the world to grow in the grace and knowledge of the Lord Jesus Christ (2 Peter 3:18). We are called to bear "one another's burdens, and so fulfill the law of Christ" (Galatians 6:2) in a humble and catholic spirit. In the words of Paul: "Let us not be weary in well doing, for in due season we shall reap, if we faint not" (Galatians 6:9).

Practicing the Apostolicity of the Church

The Church is built upon the foundation of the apostles and prophets, the cornerstone of which is Christ Jesus (Ephesians 2:20). Apostles were eye-witnesses of Jesus' ministry, death, and resurrection (Acts 1:22). They, along with prophets, were spokesmen for the Savior (John 14:26; 15:26). They wrote the Scriptures, which the Church recognized as canonical for faith and practice. The written Word of God, which testifies of the living Word, Christ Jesus, is thus the norm by which the life of the Church is to be measured. The Church can be one, holy, and catholic only insofar as she is an apostolic Church founded upon Christ alone.[35]

Christian history reflects diverse interpretations of what the apostolicity of the Church means. Roman Catholics stress an apostolic authority that is based on Scripture plus Church tradition, and is mediated through bishops and ultimately the pope, or the bishop of Rome.[36] Eastern Orthodox and

---

[35] Edmund P. Clowney, *The Church* (Downers Grove, Ill.: InterVarsity Press, 1995), pp. 73–78.

[36] The Roman Catholic argument is traceable back to Irenaeus who asserted, in an *ad hoc* fashion, an unbroken line of bishops in the church. But Irenaeus appealed to a practical principle of episcopal succession more as an argument against the gnostic claim than as a theological principle of apostolic or episcopalian succession.

Anglican churches also stress the role of the epis-
copacy in defining the apostolic church.

The Reformation reasserted Scripture alone (*sola
Scriptura*) as the true measure of apostolicity.[37] The
Reformers identified the marks of the true,
apostolic Church as the faithful preaching of the
Word, the proper administration of the sacraments,
and the faithful exercise of Church discipline. The
pattern for these marks was set by the New Testament Church in its doctrine, experience, and practice (Acts 2:42ff.). Apostolic doctrine produces
apostolic experience and apostolic living, the
Reformers said. What we often miss is the need to
conform to apostolic practice.

When Protestants say they believe in "one holy,
catholic, apostolic church," they confess that Christ,
not the church or any man, is the rock upon which
every attribute of the Church is built. Christ is the
rock of the Church's unity, sanctity, catholicity, and
apostolicity. He builds His Church by means of of-
ficebearers and apostolic doctrine.

We do not believe *in* a church, however, for that
would mean we place our trust in it. We believe

---

[37] Consequently, the Reformed tradition strove to develop a
scriptural form of church order represented by pastors, elders, and deacons. Generally speaking, Congregationalists
and Baptists placed a greater emphasis on the authority of
Christ as expressed directly through the congregation.

only in Christ. We believe only that there is a Church that is holy, catholic, and apostolic.

It takes faith to confess these attributes of the Church because we fail to see so many of them. When we gaze upon the Church's external appearance, her garments appear soiled and torn. We see disunity rather than unity, unholiness rather than holiness, denominationalism rather than catholicity, and apostasy rather than apostolicity. We see a Church that tragically withholds the gospel from people, then wonders why she has lost her audience. Cold preaching, lukewarm members, love of power, lack of discipline, worldliness, entertainment, and politics usurp the gospel. "Much that passes for New Testament Christianity is little more than objective truth sweetened with song and made palatable by religious entertainment," said A.W. Tozer.

"When recreation gets ahead of re-creation," wrote Vance Havner, "then God's house has become a den of thieves." What both the world and the Church need is "neither a Christless churchianity nor a churchless Christianity, but Christ the Head living afresh in His body, the Church," Havner added.

When we see the Church's decline from within and society's threats from without, we are tempted to say that the Church cannot survive. Nevertheless, we are not tempted to abandon her, for she, said Calvin, is our "mother." Though it appears to age and fail, we still cherish the Church. By faith, we still trust that "the Son of God, from the beginning to the end of the world, gathers, defends, and preserves by His Spirit and Word, out of the whole human race, a Church chosen to everlasting life, agreeing in true faith; and that I am and for ever shall remain, a living member thereof" (Heidelberg Catechism, Q. 54). Because the Church is Christ's bride, she cannot fail. By faith, we believe she will complete Christ's purpose for her. Jesus guarantees that success when He says, "I will build My church."

The Church's Success: The Workmanship of Christ

Some believers belong to small, weak fellowships. They struggle from year to year while attendance dwindles. No new people are attracted to the church; there are few conversions; and people seem to have lost a true sense of the presence of God. People get discouraged. They become embarrassed, apologetic—even cynical about the Church. They gradually start distancing themselves from the congregation as well as its ministries.

That slow but sure separation from the Church in response to discouragement is part of Satan's strategy. It's the same kind of thing that prompted the disciples of Christ to forsake their Master as He was led away to be crucified. To fight Satan's efforts to separate us from the Church, we must be reminded of the magnificent promise of the almighty Son of God: "I will build My Church."

The Battle against Darkness

Christ did not say, "I will try to build My Church," or "I wish I could build My Church." He said, "I *will* build My Church. I created the heavens and the earth; I have called the world from nothing by My power. I, the Almighty, will build My Church."

That is what Christ has determined to accomplish. It's His vow, backed by His authority in heaven and on earth. "Let me tell you what I will do," Christ said to Peter. "I will build My Church. And even the gates of hell will not prevail against it."

The gates of hell (or Hades) lead to more than death. They lead to all the powers of darkness and evil. Jesus sees Hades, as it were, as an organized city with gates. A city gate in the ancient world was the place where judgment and wisdom were dispensed by the elders and rulers of the city. So what Jesus refers to here is what Paul describes in Ephesians 6:10–20 as the powers of darkness organized to destroy the people and kingdom of God. Jesus thus says that though the Church is built in a context of cosmic spiritual antithesis, which is rife with the conflict promised in Genesis 3:15 and pursued through the ages, it will not founder before the gates of the enemy. Christ's Church may lose many skirmishes, but she will win the great battle. Christ is stronger than Satan; therefore His Church will defeat Satan's army. The Seed of the woman shall prevail over the seed of the serpent.

That statement must have seemed preposterous to the handful of nobodies who followed Jesus. Yet Jesus looked at the fishermen, tax collector, and other disciples and promised, "Upon this rock I will build My Church, and the gates of hell shall not prevail against it."

What seemed so preposterous has happened, and is still happening. Throughout history, even when the Church seemed overwhelmed by the powers of darkness, she has survived and grown. "God in the midst of her doth dwell," John Flavel admonished people who were quick to mourn a faltering church. "Be not too quick to bury the church before she be dead."

The Church may stagger, but she will surely continue her march through history to ultimate triumph. That is because Jesus Christ guarantees her success. He will never dismiss her as irrelevant, as others do. Individual churches may close their doors, denominations may wither, but the Church of Christ will grow and prosper. As the Belgic Confession (Article 27) says, "This holy church is preserved or supported by God against the rage of the whole world, even though she sometimes (for a while) appears very small and—in the eyes of men—to be reduced to nothing, as during the perilous reign of Ahab the Lord reserved unto Him seven thousand men who had not bowed their knees to Baal."

If we truly grasped God's perspective of the Church, many of the problems we struggle with in the local church would seem so small. Consider, for example, that while Israel saw only the rubbish of Jerusalem, God saw rebuilt walls (Isaiah 49:16). When we see a Church torn by dissension, God sees a glorious Church elected by the Father (Ephesians 1:3–6), redeemed by the Son (Ephesians 1:7), and adopted by the Spirit (Romans 8:15). She is glorious because of her role in the plan of God (Ephesians 3:10–11), her holiness (Ephesians 2:10), her access to God (Hebrews 4:16), and her distinguished inheritance (Ephesians 1:14, 18). As John Newton wrote:

> *Glorious things of thee are spoken,*
> *Zion, city of our God,*

> He whose word cannot be broken
> Formed thee for His own abode:
> On the Rock of Ages founded,
> What can shake thy sure repose?
> With salvation's walls surrounded,
> Thou mayst smile at all thy foes.

A Work under Construction

True Christians are members of the only successful institution on earth. "No group, no movement, no institution of any kind in the world can even approach to the glory, the splendour, the honour, the beauty, the magnificence, the wonder, the dignity, the excellence, the resplendency of the church of God," writes Daniel Wray.[38] We should serve the Church, and Christ through the Church, with all our hearts, always remembering that our labor is not in vain in the Lord (1 Corinthians 15:58). Once we grasp this, we can confess with Timothy Dwight:

> I love Thy church, O God!
> Her walls before Thee stand,
> Dear as the apple of Thine eye,
> And graven on Thy hand.

---

[38] *The Importance of the Local Church* (Edinburgh: Banner of Truth Trust, 1981), pp. 4–7. Cf. Kuiper, *The Glorious Body of Christ*; à Brakel, *The Christian's Reasonable Service*, 2:58–60.

For her my tears shall fall,
For her my prayers ascend,
To her my cares and toils be given,
Till toils and cares shall end.

The Church is a fleet of fishing boats, not a yachting club; a hospital for sinners, not a museum for saints. We dedicate our lives to a work in progress: to what Christ has promised and paid for with His own blood; to what is worthwhile and shall be successful in the end, though there will always be dross amid the gold. The Church's work, therefore, is never in vain. It is the product of God's sovereign grace in Christ, not the product of the mind and efforts of men.

Christ's promise that He will build the Church is already being fulfilled. But on this side of the Day of Judgment, the Church is under construction. And, like any building site, this place of construction isn't necessarily tidy or impressive. It includes piles of bricks and boards, ugly trenches, waste, rubble, and abandoned tools.

If we look at that mess, we can easily become discouraged. We see so many unfinished people in the Church who are full of imperfections and weakness. If we think we're going to find something better than that, we only set ourselves up for disappointment. Instead of criticizing people who fall short of our expectations, however, we ought to put on our boots, overalls, and helmets, and get busy on the work site.

We should also prepare ourselves for a lot of hard work that may not seem to get much accomplished. Regardless, *ora et labora* ("pray and work!") must become our song. "The church of Christ needs servants of all kinds, and instruments of every sort; penknives as well as swords, axes as well as hammers, Marthas as well as Marys, Peters as well as Johns," wrote J. C. Ryle. Though we'll struggle with many challenges and experience much discomfort along the way, we ought to press on, always remembering what the Church is going to be some day—a bride adorned for her husband, without spot or wrinkle. "The church shall survive the world, and be in bliss when that is in ruins," wrote Matthew Henry. "When men are projecting the church's ruin, God is preparing for its salvation."

Finally, before we complain about the messiness of the Church's building site, we should think about the growing process of every believer. Isn't every one of us under construction? Some of us aren't very impressive yet; we have a long way to go. Our faith, which may be true faith, is not very strong. But little strings are needed as much as big strings in God's concert of grace. "Christians in concert are an abridgment of heaven, shining like a firmament of bright stars," George Swinnock wrote.

The work of the Church may be small in our eyes, but it is Christ's work, and will abide forever. As Builder and Maker, God will not rest until His city is complete. The Church chosen from eternity past will glorify the triune God forever. Christ shall lose none of those given to Him by the Father, chosen to everlasting life (John 17:12). The Church is the only institution in the world that never loses its members, even by death.

One day Christ's work will also be finished in us, and our Bridegroom will present us to His Father in glory, sanctified and perfected by His work in us. When we pass from the militant to the triumphant Church, all sorrow will be forgotten, all sighing will flee, and we shall forever praise the Lamb who sits on the throne. As John Murray concluded, "It is both the privilege and obligation of believers to appreciate more and more the complementation of Christ and His church."[39]

I believe there is a holy, catholic, apostolic, and eternal Church, built and maintained by Jesus Christ on the solid rock of Peter's confession: "Thou art the Christ, the Son of the living God" (Matthew 16:16). I believe in the perseverance of the saints and of the Church because I believe in the

---

[39] *Collected Writings,* 1:244.

perseverance of the Christ of God. "The church is nothing but Christ displayed," wrote William Gurnall. And He will not forsake the work of His own hands.

"Christ is the King of His church, and the church is the greatest queen in the world," said Richard Sibbes. Let us therefore keep courage and cherish the Church for Christ's sake, for she is heir to His cross and His glory.

> *Mount Zion, glorious and fair,*
> *Gives joy to people in all lands;*
> *The city of the mighty King*
> *In majesty securely stands.*
>
> *Within her dwellings for defense*
> *Our God has made His presence known,*
> *And hostile kings, in sudden fear,*
> *Have fled as ships by tempests blown.*
>
> *With our own eyes we have beheld*
> *What oft our fathers told before,*
> *That God Who in His Zion dwells*
> *Will keep her safely ever more.*[40]

---

[40] *The Psalter* (Grand Rapids, Mich.: Eerdmans, 1927), Psalm 131, stanzas 2–4.

Glorious things of thee are spoken,
Zion, city of our God;
He whose word cannot be broken
Formed thee for His own abode.
On the Rock of Ages founded,
What can shake thy sure repose?
With salvation's walls surrounded,
Thou mayst smile at all thy foes.

John Newton

On the Rock
of Ages Founded

Jonathan Gerstner on the Marks of a True Church

Asia Minor, during the first century A.D., was in the midst of a violent struggle. On the one side was an apparently ancient assembly of believers with history on their side; on the other side was an apparently new movement with scarcely any members of the historic establishment. Yet God had a different view of which group was in fact His assembly.

Satan is the expert on counterfeits. He is a liar and the father of lies (John 8:44). Yet the saddest counterfeit he has been able to produce is his counterfeit church. Already in the book of Revelation, the Spirit of God encourages suffering believers with the truth that the institutional persecution they were receiving was not coming from the true assembly of God, but rather from "those who say they are Jews and are not, but are a synagogue of Satan" (Revelation 2:9; 3:9). These words of the risen Christ are in sharp contrast to the attitude which many who profess His name today express about organized churches. Few in this politically correct age would feel comfortable with a teacher who charged that the religion called Judaism is actually a confederation of synagogues of Satan. Fewer still in our compromised church world would feel comfortable with acknowledging the organization headed by the Pope of Rome as a false and apostate church.

Yet the Word of God clearly establishes that there are assemblies which, though daring to claim the name of "church" or "synagogue" which are not drawn together by God, but by Satan himself. Here, of course, we are speaking about the church assembled here on the earth, often called "the visible church." God has His own spiritual church, chosen in Christ before the foundation of the earth. From this body there will be no falling away. But God also established an institutionalized church on this earth. This visible church has true and false members, and the organization itself can be, and has been, taken over by Satan so as to be no longer God's assembly, but that of the Evil One, leaving behind a true remnant as the true visible church.

Indeed, Satan could think of no better place to have unbelievers than in a counterfeit church that claims the name of God while denying His gospel and ignoring Christ's Lordship. "Synagogues of Satan" are sometimes called "apostate" (that is, fallen) churches. To be apostate, a church must have at one time professed the true religion and now must have fallen to the point that it denies the faith. At the time of the greatest apostasy to date in the visible church, the death of the Roman Catholic Church as a true church, the most common term used by biblical believers was "the false church." Concern over this peril was the foundation of the warning stated in a great creed of the Reformation, the Belgic Confession (1561). In Article 29, it concludes its presentation of the true church and the false church with the following powerful affirmation: "These two churches are easily known and distinguished from each other." These prophetic words also seem sadly like a word from bygone times. Yet Jesus Christ's jealousy for His Church remains the same yesterday, today and forever.

Besides his ploy of counterfeiting the Church, Satan has excelled in causing true churches of Christ to be smashed into countless splinters. In an alleged attempt to produce a pure form of the true church, more and more persons have started congregations and denominations on their own initiative. Most people decide to join a church based upon finding a place where they feel "at home." But it is clear from even a cursory study of Scripture that many will feel comfortable in places that are not true churches at all. People seem more and more comfortable accepting, as the one mark of a church, "a place where I feel comfortable," indeed, like the pub of television fame, a place "where everybody knows your name."

Even individuals who otherwise show remarkable doctrinal perceptiveness seem quite at peace saying, "My church began in 1972," or "My church dates back to 1830." If a "church" began in a certain year it is, by definition, actually a cult. The true visible church, according to Scripture, began in Eden. The dispensational claim that the church began at Pentecost is totally false. One church did begin in the first century A.D. This church which began around A.D. 70, with the destruction of the temple in Jerusalem, was a false church. The cut-off branches from the olive tree which Paul discussed in Romans 11 were united together in their satanic apostasy to form synagogues of Satan, claiming the Old Testament Scriptures while denying the Messiah. If our church began at any time after Eden, not standing in covenant continuity with God's covenant people, we are a cult.

Each true church must be able to trace its history back to Eden and explain every apparent separation as in fact a falling away of the other body from the faith. If not, we are guilty of the sin of schism, and must repent and seek reunion with the bodies from which we have separated, unless they have in the meantime in fact apostatized. One irony of history is that churches have left other bodies schismatically, but the absence of the departing brothers and sisters has in some cases hastened the doctrinal departure of those remaining. So the departing brothers are guilty of schism, but in the meantime the mother body from which they had no biblical right to separate has in fact apostatized. So the formerly schismatic body, when convicted of its sin, is a little like a sinful spouse who deserted his partner without biblical grounds, has been converted, and now seeks reconciliation with the former spouse, only to learn it is too late for that former mate has remarried. In this fallen world, the original marriage cannot be restored, but still schism, like unbiblical divorce, must be confessed.

God Himself established the visible church when He preached the gospel to Adam and Eve. Christ renewed the Church by purchasing its redemption in space and time, and sending the Spirit to equip all believers. Christ also gave the visible church even more organizational structure through appointing apostles as church officers and outlining steps for church discipline. Those assemblies who apostatize, that is, lose the marks of the true church, are the ones who begin a new existence apart from God's ordained visible church. Any true church must be able to trace its history back to the visible church which God has established in Scripture, and show that any separations were the result of apostasy, not a schismatic spirit.

The call to remain in spiritually sick visible churches is very unpopular today, when virtually all are seeking churches to meet one's own needs. So quickly the command of Scripture to maintain the unity of the Spirit in the bonds of peace (Ephesians 4:3) becomes passed off as a mere exhortation to maintain a spiritual unity that ignores the organizational unity ordered when Christ equipped His visible church from the beginning with officers and structure. My late father, Dr. John H. Gerstner, agonized before coming to the conclusion that the church he had given most of his life to purify was now apostate. He grieved also to find people in his new communion talking about splitting the body over such neutral matters as styles of music used in worship. How alien to the modern church world is the vivid picture in Dante's *Inferno* of the schismatic. He is pictured as condemned eternally to rip apart his own bowels as a just punishment for the way in which he ripped apart the Church of Christ. Indeed, schism may have become the forgotten sin of the twentieth-century church.

Already the Belgic Confession noted the danger of this opposite extreme. It grants the existence of hypocrites "who are mixed in the [true visible] church with the good" (Article 29), and notes that "those who separate themselves from the same [i.e., the true visible church] or do not join themselves to it act contrary to the ordinance of God" (Article 28). This beautiful balance between ignoring apostasy and promoting schism is amplified further in that great Puritan document, the Westminster Confession (1646): "The purest churches under heaven are subject to mixture and error; and some have so degenerated as to become no churches of Christ, but synagogues of Satan" (Article 25, section 5). In this fallen world there is no truly pure church. Yet in this fallen world there are true churches, which we must join and maintain fellowship with, and false churches with which maintaining fellowship is a denial of Christ.

Visible, Not Invisible Church

The Scripture powerfully presents the reality of true and false manifestations of the church on this earth. The visible church or Israel is presented in a powerful image as an olive tree in Romans 11. With regard to God's eternal decree, only the elect are members of the spiritual church, the invisible church. "Not all of Israel are Israel" (Romans 9:6). Augustine wisely noted that some of those within (the visible church) are, in fact, without (the invisible church). But the visible church, represented by the olive tree of Romans 11, experiences a constant adding to and cutting off of branches. What clearer picture can we have of God's care for the visible church than that branches of the tree can and have been cut off? To be a member of a true church, one must be engrafted into a true part of this visible olive tree, which has roots in space and time that reach all the way back to Eden.

The Splintering of the True Church

Biblical ecclesiology would be much easier for all believers to grasp if at the time of the Reformation one unified, true, evangelical, catholic (universal), visible church had been formed in contrast to the false catholic church of Rome. However, the very decay of the Middle Ages made that impossible. Biblical church government had ceased to exist for at least 1000 years. When the Reformation came there were no unified biblical assemblies of elders to oversee the smooth transition caused by the falling away of the false church. Instead, and with particular irony, disagreement over the sacraments, given to express the unity of the body, became an issue of separation. Simply put, no one branch, Reformed, Lutheran, or Anabaptist, could accept the other's view as tolerable. So the trunk of the olive tree divided in three ways as part of the aftermath of the late medieval apostasy. The marks of this basic division are borne by the evangelical churches even today.

Each church, regardless from which of the three

segments it was born, must maintain the marks of a true church and not view itself as independent from the historic development of Christ's visible church. For any branch of the church to forbid membership to those who differ with their view of the sacraments is sectarian. If one is a member of the body of Christ, he must be able to be a member of any true visible church. However, while granting an appropriate latitude in non-essential beliefs to members who will abide under the authority of the elders of the church, any church must also require a higher standard of doctrinal fidelity from officers of the church, based on its understanding of important doctrines like the sacraments. Scripture requires that an overseer of the church must be able to teach, and one cannot be a teacher who knows only the milk of basic Christianity (1 Timothy 3:2; Hebrews 5:12). Since, sadly, disagreement remains among true Christian churches about non-essential but important aspects of the meat of the Word, elders and pastors cannot be simply exchanged between all true churches.

True Church, Not Pure Church

With these things in mind, a key doctrinal point must be grasped in order rightly to discern which are true visible churches of God today. The Scripture calls us to discern true churches, not pure churches. There are no truly pure churches in this fallen world. The confusion of true church and pure church is at least as old as the Donatist controversy of the early church, and it was revived in the Anabaptist movement of Reformation times. When one confuses true church and pure church, one is doomed to a series of schisms as each new manifestation reveals its own impurity.

The rejection of purity as the criterion to judge which is a true church also follows explicitly from the teaching of Scripture. Christ commanded believers to listen to the Pharisees when they sat in Moses' seat, even as He warned them not to follow their impure, hypocritical lifestyle (Matthew 23:2). Christ went to the synagogue on every Sabbath as was His custom (Luke 4:16). The same leaders and their disciples would, in a generation, lead these churches into becoming synagogues of Satan, and already had the spirit of apostasy working in their hearts; but until that visible church became apostate, believers were required to remain.

Purifying the True Church

At this point in the discussion we must already be very careful not to misunderstand the call to judge the visible church of God by the criteria of true and false churches as a rejection of the church's call to purity. An absolute requirement of

all Christians is to do all in their power to work by
godly means to purify the visible church. The
Puritans typified this holy calling of refining with
all their might, while also refusing to separate from
the visible church. They recognized that the impurity that remains in the visible church is a foothold
for Satan to destroy it, and to turn it into a synagogue of Satan. We are not surprised when we see
the hypocritical Pharisees eventually betray the role
of sitting in the seat of Moses by denying the
proven Messiah Moses had predicted. The corrupt
medieval church quickly gave way to become the
apostate Church of Rome at the Council of Trent.
The passion to present a pure bride to Christ
(Ephesians 5:26–27) must remain, even though
Christ Himself warned that such purity would
never be attained in this world.

The Marks of the True Church

How do we tell the true and false churches
apart? By God's grace He has placed clear marks
in His true church. When the Reformers wrestled
with this question, they generally came up with
three key marks. The Belgic Confession again is
particularly helpful: "The marks by which the true
Church is known are these: *If the pure doctrine of the
Gospel is preached therein,* if it maintains the pure
administration of the sacraments as instituted by

Christ, if church discipline is exercised in the punishing of sin; *in short, if all things are managed according to the pure Word of God, all things contrary thereto rejected, and Jesus Christ acknowledged as the only Head of the Church"* (Article 29; emphasis mine).

My personal conviction is that in fact there are two marks, as the final clause of the quotation from the Belgic Confession suggests. The second and third of the classic three are in fact applications of the more basic second mark. These two basic marks are the proclamation of the true Gospel and acknowledgment of the Lordship of Christ exercised through His Word. The proper administration of the sacraments and church discipline are sub-elements inherent in the second mark, and may never be compromised. However, these two applications were particularly emphasized in light of the current manifestation of apostasy in the false church of the time. There are many more applications of the second mark as well. Any time an ecclesiological organization flaunts Christ by flaunting His Word, it reveals itself to be a false church.

Preaching the True Gospel

Clearly one cannot have a true church without the gospel. The entire book of Galatians is dedicated to that central theme. The beautiful vision given in Revelation 1 of the church depicted as lampstands shining in a dark world includes the somber warning of Christ that He may sovereignly take away the light from an offending church. Churches without the Gospel generally maintain organizational structure. On the surface nothing has changed, but in God's eyes they have ceased to be true churches and have become false ones. This change can also be perceived by discerning believers who see that the proclamation of the Gospel is gone, and that now all that is left is Satan's synagogue.

The Lordship of Christ as Expressed in Scripture as the Second Mark of the Church

The view that the Lordship of Christ as expressed in Scripture is in fact the second mark of a true church in no way lessens the significance of the second and third traditional marks (right administration of sacraments and church discipline). Rather it establishes them, given the indisputable biblical character of these marks. However, it leaves open the wide biblical scope of any area that Christ commands decisively through Scripture. All such truths are requisite marks of the true church as well.

The Lordship of Christ is an undeniable mark of a true church. Whose church is it after all? For the false church the answer is simple: it is the church of the denominational hierarchies or the people in the pew. For the true church, it is Christ's church, and parishioners and clergy alike bow before Him and His direction as given for eternity in Holy Scripture.

The Sacraments

Understanding the second mark as acknowledging the Lordship of Christ as revealed in Scripture helps undo some of the division which occurred among true believers after the Reformation. If, for example, a church wrongly, in the conviction of this author, believes that baptism ought to be given to adult professing believers only, this belief does not necessarily render it a false church. If the church of this opinion in fact believes it is following the teaching of Scripture, it has not violated the second mark.

If, however, the church were convinced that the covenantal perspective that children of believers ought to be incorporated into the church by baptism is faithful to Scripture, but out of tradition refused to bow to Scripture, it would in fact be a false church. As the Belgic Confession pointed out, not only were the true sacraments distorted, but the false church brazenly had added other sacraments to its practice. The issue of apostasy was the refusal of the church to bow before the Scripture's teaching concerning the sacraments, not an honest mistake in interpreting the Scripture by a church which loved its Lord.

Discipline

The doctrine of church discipline has a twofold significance. First, the true church recognizes its moral responsibility to Christ to exercise biblical church discipline over professing church members and pastors who live in moral and doctrinal sin. The failure to strive to maintain discipline reveals an arrogant refusal to acknowledge that the church is in fact God's church, not a social club for seminary classmates and family.

The corollary point provides a visible evidence of when a body is a false church. Generally, the apostate body will in fact falsely discipline those who work to purify its errors. One can make a strong case that any body that removes or forbids candidates from serving as ministers because these ministers are proclaiming the truth is in fact an apostate body.

Error and Apostasy

This leads us to the excruciatingly difficult areas of applying these marks of the true church in the light of the biblically explained and experientially observed impurity of all churches. All of us are prone to error. Thus true churches can and do fall into error. Clearly, if the error amounts to a repudiation of the Gospel, these churches have become apostate. Two contemporary issues being debated even in professing evangelical circles are annihilationism and salvation outside of Christ. Annihilationism denies the eternality of hell. It thus, by irrefutable implication, denies the seriousness of the atonement, for Christ purchased redemption to cover the penalty of sin. If all that is owed God for sin is physical death, all Christ had to do was to physically die and not bear the eternal wrath of God for believers. So the cross, the very heart of the Gospel, is demeaned. Similarly, if one dares against Scripture to conjecture the salvation of an adult person who has never heard the Gospel, salvation no longer comes through faith in the proclamation of the Gospel alone. A church which affirms either of these errors against the foundation of the Gospel reveals itself to be false.

The second mark, the acknowledgment of the Lordship of Christ as expressed in the teaching of Scripture, is harder to apply. If an error does not directly undercut the Gospel, it still may fall within the category of refusing to regulate all things according to the Word. Here an honest and prayerful decision is to be made.

For example, at the time of the Reformation both sides in the controversy saw the difference between covenantal and professing believers' baptism as involving such a serious error that one could not honestly take the opposing position without intentionally flaunting Scripture. Today almost all evangelical leaders are equally convinced that people and churches differ here without desiring to flaunt Scripture. As they see it, those who hold the alternative view are erroneous, but are not in violation of the second mark of a true church. They would be true churches in error.

On the other hand, there is universal agreement among churches holding to biblical Christianity that the defense of homosexuality as a Christian option is an intentional twisting of Scripture to defend the culture's values. Therefore a church which defends such doctrine is a false church.

Some cases fall in the middle. Believers who agree that it is unbiblical to ordain women are sincerely divided about whether the defense of the practice proves an apostate denial of indisputable biblical teaching, or a serious though misguided attempt at honest biblical exegesis. So in a biblical ecclesiology one must not merely look to the truth of a position, but also to the manner in which it is argued to see if one has a true church in error or a false church.

The two foundational marks of a true church thus establish that in fact there are many more subsidiary marks than just three. Any time a church openly flaunts the authority of Christ, it has become apostate. If it still formally worships Him with the lips, it is still a visible church, though its heart remains far from Christ. As our Lord taught His followers, we must listen to the Pharisees when they sit in Moses' seat, even though just a few decades later they would become part of an apostate church for denying that the Messiah had come.

This leads to the distinction between the *esse* (being) and *bene esse* (well-being) of the church. Maintaining these basic principles is necessary to even being a true church at all. For the health and well-being of the church, working out these principles is the key. Every error harms the *bene esse* of the church, but by God's grace not all errors destroy the *esse* or there would be no true church left on the earth, given the universality of sin and error in a fallen world.

Similarly, one of the hardest points of agony over apostasy is the distinction between *de facto* (in reality) and *de jure* (by law) apostasy. *De jure* apostasy is clear-cut. The organization explicitly denies one or both of the two marks. Three open-and-shut cases in church history are Judaism, Roman Catholicism, and the Unitarian-Universalist com-

munion. Judaism, as we see documented in
Scripture, is an apostate body which formally rejects both the Gospel and the Lordship of Christ.
Roman Catholicism equally repudiated the Gospel
explicitly at the Council of Trent (1545–1563) when
it taught, "If anyone sayeth that by faith alone the
impious [unrighteous] are justified . . . let him be
anathema" (Canon VII on justification). The
Unitarian-Universalist communion came into existence by formerly faithful congregational churches
attacking the deity of Christ and, hence, His
Lordship.

The question then comes whether one ought to
leave a church which has not yet formally repudiated the Gospel or Christ's Lordship, but yet in
practice evidences the same. This concept of *de
facto* apostasy is much harder to tackle, and must
be approached with prayerful caution. This distinction can be abused by those who schismatically
want to leave an erring but true church. On the
other side, however, it appears that a real apostasy
can in some cases exist without *de jure* proclama-
tions of apostasy. For example, suppose that a
church claims to acknowledge the Lordship of
Christ as expressed in Scripture, and its Book of
Church Order has lengthy sections outlining how
church discipline is to be exercised, yet nevertheless, in spite of open and flagrant lives of immoral-

ity evidenced in the congregation, not one person is in fact put under the discipline of the church. Now, if the church actually outlined in its constitution that it was in principle opposed to church discipline, it would be a false church *de jure*. Has its constant failure to act rendered it a false church *de facto*? These issues must give any biblical Christian serious pause to prayerfully reflect.

When should I leave a church? The sadly common answer is "when I am fed up with fighting." This answer fails to acknowledge that in this world the church will always have corruption to be fought against. The only church in which godly members no longer vigorously contend for the truth against the introduction of error is the church triumphant in heaven. The only biblical answer is that one must leave when a church has forfeited the marks or enforced false discipline against one's conscience. The difficulty in discerning how the marks apply in difficult cases must not detract from the objective biblical criteria they provide for making a choice. For a more thorough treatment of this question, I refer you to my father's chapter at the end of this book, entitled "When A Person Must Leave a Church."

Local Church or Denomination
Some will respond to this issue of true and false

churches by saying that they are members of a local church, not a denomination. What the denomination they are a part of, does, they propose, has no impact on their role in a local congregation.

Any biblical Christian will grant that ideally there would be only one evangelical and true church. But the serious disagreement primarily about the sacraments forced bodies of churches to decide where to draw lines in the sand. Denominations and families of churches are attempts by biblical Christians in a fallen world to keep as much of the trunk of the olive tree united as possible. They are clearly closer to the biblical model of a universal visible church than isolated independent congregations.

Indeed, if one's church is strictly independent, one must explain how one's church is related to the historic church founded in Scripture. He faces the impossible task of attempting to show how one legitimately is separated from earlier biblical manifestations of the true church that involved extracongregational councils (Acts 15).

In any case, to claim one is only a member of a local church and not responsible for the conduct of one's denomination or fellowship of churches is a false and deluded observation. I am convinced that the biblical model of the church mandates the existence of assemblies of higher authority than the local congregation. This view is generally called Presbyterianism. (By the way, much of what is contemporarily called Presbyterianism is in fact elder-ruled Congregationalism, but that is for another discussion.) However, even if I were a defender of Congregationalism, the view that there is no higher spiritual authority on earth than that vested in the congregation, I would still need to defend my denominational affiliation, or lack of it.

By minimal definition, one recognizes that those who are in a denomination acknowledge each other as visible members of the body of Christ. If one's denomination tolerates those who openly flaunt the Lordship of Christ or deny the Gospel, one's membership in the denomination is giving a public statement that these apostates are nevertheless legitimately part of a visible true church. No church or family of churches is truly pure, but when the gospel and Lordship of Christ are flaunted, the assembly is no longer a true visible church, but a false church. No believer may have fellowship with a synagogue of Satan.

Fellowship and Apostasy

The ecumenical movement continues to raise a challenge for all believers who are serious about true and false churches. Assemblies such as the National and World Councils of Churches indisputably include false churches, discerned to be such when the two biblical marks are applied. If a true church is affiliated with such assemblies, it must unambiguously be made clear this church is in no way in fellowship with all member churches, but merely discussing matters with other organizations who at some point in their history have had Christian roots. It would be interesting to see if these ecumenical agencies would tolerate member churches who speak that truth so boldly. If, however, one remains in these bodies as a mark of fellowship with all member churches, that church may legitimately be declared apostate. For example, both mentioned bodies have denominations that affirm the practicing homosexual lifestyle as an appropriate Christian lifestyle. A church that might in other regards appear to be a true church is therefore renouncing the Lordship of Christ as expressed in Scripture, for it is refusing to heed the Apostle Paul's admonition not to even eat with immoral people who claim the name of Christ (2 Corinthians 6:11–18). It is thus shown to be a false church by its ecumenical fellowship.

If only twentieth-century evangelicals had kept this simple principle of no fellowship with those who are members of false churches, we would likely have been spared the horrible anguish caused by two documents which I believe to be apostate: "Evangelicals and [Roman] Catholics Together" and "The Gift of Salvation." These documents both compromise the necessity of the first mark of the true church, the Gospel of justification by faith alone. In the first place, the professing evangelical signatories ought never to have sat in a room and had fellowship with individuals who formerly professed to be evangelicals, but had apostatized to unite with the Roman Catholic Church. If this principle had been maintained, the initial document never would have been signed, for key Roman Catholic participants were apostate Protestants. Those who signed the second document should never have had fellowship with those formerly professing evangelicals who signed "Evangelicals and [Roman] Catholics Together." If so separated, they would never have fallen into signing "The Gift of Salvation." So, as in a line of dominoes, the evangelical failure to stand up against apostasy has resulted in an ever-deepening crisis in evangelicalism itself.

This leads to the reality of false or apostate evangelicalism. The same principles which are to be applied to denominations or congregations certainly need to be applied to this movement which claims the name of the gospel, Evangelicalism. The issue of apostate evangelicalism is the most urgent crisis facing the true church of the 21st century.

J. Gresham Machen had the ecclesiological discernment both to break with apostasy and to lead other true churches into battle with liberalism, even while knowing he differed with them on very important issues. How we pray that discerning leaders will rally the remnant of true evangelicalism to take a stand in the encircling gloom of deepening apostasy.

Fellowship and Schism

What about schismatic churches? Must we acknowledge them as false churches? Here again, the key principle is whether they intentionally separated out of their own selfish desires, or because they erroneously believed that God wanted them to separate. If it is the latter, one can gladly acknowledge that this is a true church in error about ecclesiology, and just as much a true church as a church with an erroneous view of the sacraments which is trying to serve Christ. If a church left, however, due to rebellious attitudes against Christ Himself (such as, for example, the sadly common case of a pastor schismatically starting a new church to avoid biblical discipline by his fellow elders), we must acknowledge it as a false church and refuse to have fellowship with it.

Conclusion

This has been a difficult article to write. It is easy to develop an unbiblical fear of Satan when we see how much he has accomplished, sowing tares in God's wheat field, by creating false churches. We must remember that the Lord of the Church will preserve the Church. The false church in the 16th century was so strong that it took the life of Guido de Bres, the chief author of the Belgic Confession, not long after the words were penned. Still his faithful interpretation of Scripture is here being presented afresh to believers for guidance into the 21st century.

I am convinced that some who read this article will realize they must leave their current ecclesiastical organization. They must join a true church that is faithful to the Gospel and subject to the Lordship of Christ as revealed in the Scripture. Others will realize that they have divorced their church in haste, and now realize it to be an ailing but true church of Christ. They will need humbly to return. Perhaps the greatest providential irony of this article is that not a day goes by in which I do not agonize over these very points as I assess the state of my own denominational home in light of the very criteria on which I have written this article.

Many sadly trivialize church membership as no more than being part of a club. I once heard a dear sister in the Lord bewailing a church schism, apparently because it divided the family at a family reunion. The Church is Christ's church, and faithfulness to Christ requires us to join, just as faithfulness to Christ requires us to leave when it is no longer a true church.

The Dutch church leader Philip Hoedemaker, in the midst of anguished examination of his own denomination at the turn of the twentieth century, is noted for having said, "The church is your mother. If your mother is a prostitute, you still don't leave your mother." This is a very powerful image, and a wise admonition against schism. However, if your mother is dead, she is dead. Satan may have reanimated the corpse with the appearance of life, but she is still dead. May the Lord give us all wisdom to know when we serve to purify an impure mother, and when we have, through our own sentimentality, started to serve Satan.

Blest be the tie that binds
Our hearts in Christian love;
The fellowship of kindred minds
Is like to that above.

John Fawcett

Blest Be the Tie That Binds

Don Kistler on Church Membership

When the Apostle Paul spoke of the Church in the New Testament, he availed himself of a metaphor which had not previously been used: the body of Christ. In previous times the Church had been called "My people," "The Israel of God," "the called-out ones" (*ecclesia*), but never Christ's body; that is a novel term of Pauline usage. The apostle wrote in Ephesians that we are "members of His body." The unfolding of history, then, is the outworking of how Christ adds members to His body until that body is complete, at which time history will have reached its fulfillment. Salvation engrafts new members into the body of Christ, each having their own distinct role and function.

When we speak of the Church, we often speak of it in two ways: the visible church and the invisible Church. The visible church is that group of professed believers who have joined themselves to local bodies which are recognized to be "Christian." In this group there will be "wheat and tares," true believers and false believers (who appear to be true because of their profession). The invisible Church is that congregation of all true believers; its membership is ultimately known only to God Himself, who alone can judge the heart, its motives, and the sincerity of a person's profession. When a person becomes a true Christian, he is automatically made a member of the invisible Church (all true believers). It stands to reason, then, that this person would also automatically desire to become a member of that which is the visible manifestation of that reality, the local church.

In our individualistic, pluralistic, relativistic day, we often hear such claims as "Church membership is nowhere addressed in Scripture." Or, "God doesn't care if you're a member of a church or not, as long as you love Him." These and other similar claims, I believe, are false, and show a gross ignorance of biblical teaching. I also believe that church membership is easily deduced and proven by "Scripture and evident reason."

God wants His people to be members of a local church. Is there a verse of Scripture that says, "Be ye members of a local church"? No, I grant, no such verse exists. But if we ask the question, "Is there good reason and inference from Scripture that God expects professing believers to hold their membership in a local body?" the answer is a resounding "YES!"

This stance assumes and presumes a doctrine of the local church as well as a doctrine of the universal Church. The Church is comprised of all be-

lievers of all times, who are joined and united by
Christ into Christ, and who are joined and united
to each other in the essentials, the non-negotiables,
of the Christian faith in this life, and who will be
joined and united in *all* matters of the Christian
faith in the life to come.

There is a tendency among some to denigrate
the local church. They believe that, as long as they
are members of the universal Church, belonging to
a local church is optional. I believe the message of
the Bible is opposed to such a position, and will
provide the following reasons for such a conclusion:

The New Testament churches were local, visible
churches. They met in specific places. Matthew
18:20 speaks of as few as two or three gathering together in Christ's name. Acts 11:26 tells us that the
church in Antioch, where the disciples were first
called "Christians," assembled together for the purpose of being taught. Paul wrote his epistles to specific churches in specific locations, with pastors
and elders (or overseers) shepherding their flocks.

The local church is God's tool for bringing His
people to full maturity in knowledge and faith.
Ephesians 4:11–13: "He gave some as pastors and
teachers, for the equipping of the saints for the
work of service, to the building up of the body of
Christ; until we all attain to the unity of the faith,

and to the knowledge of the Son of God, to a mature man" (NASB). It is not an invisible, floating, ethereal body of believers; rather, it is an actual place with an actual pastor and teachers, who are equipping saints for the work of service to the body of Christ.

Certainly the Great Commission (Matthew 28:18–20) points to church membership. If a person is to be baptized, which is a sacrament of the church, someone who is commissioned by a church body to administer that sacrament would be required to do so. That person is an ordained elder of the church, someone who is qualified and commissioned to be a "steward of the mysteries of God." Now on what basis would such an elder baptize someone with whom there was no relationship? Persons are to be discipled, they are to be baptized, and they are to be taught to be obedient. Obedient to what? To God's Word! As defined and interpreted by whom? By an ordained elder of a duly constituted church body.

Additionally, Christ said that He would build His Church. Obviously Christ was not referring to "The First Baptist Church" or "Second Presbyterian Church." He was speaking of the true Church, comprised of all true members of Christ's mystical body. But those members of His body meet somewhere; they are taught somewhere; they worship together somewhere; and when they do so they are a local manifestation of the larger reality of Christ's Church, His Body. Even in a denomination, the local church is only a neighborhood manifestation of the larger denomination. It is not the denomination; it is an area's or city's local representation of the denomination. And for that reason we call it "the local church." The point is, however, that the true Christian wants to be a part of what Christ is building, which is His Church. He wants to manifest his association with Christ and His Church in any and every way possible.

Last, the Church is one of two organisms divinely instituted by God for the spreading of His love and His gospel. One is the church; the other is the family. Membership is not optional in either one. By virtue of being physically alive, we are members of a particular family. We are not simply members of "the family of man," but we are also members of an individual, specific, local family. By virtue of being spiritually alive—born again or regenerated—we are members of the invisible Church, the family of God, and therefore must join ourselves with the actual reality of that concept, namely the local church.

The Old Testament practice of membership certainly shows the importance of this affiliation. Being an Israelite was not simply an issue of race and nationality, but an issue of being in covenant bond with God. Romans 9:6: "For they are not all Israel who are descended from Israel." What made someone a true Israelite was his relationship with the living God, not his relationship to his parents or ancestors.

God commanded circumcision as the sign of acceptance into the covenant community (Genesis 17:7–10). In fact, God nearly killed Moses for not circumcising his male child. Abraham was not a Jew by birth, but by circumcision. Baptism is now the New Testament sign of acceptance into the covenant community (Colossians 2:11). There was not only to be an inward reality, a circumcision of the heart, but an outward sign of that invisible reality. Time and time again God calls for an outward show of what has happened internally. Good works do not save, but they are visible evidence that a work of grace has taken place in the heart. Baptism does not save, but it is visible evidence of an inward reality. Church membership does not save, but it is visible evidence of being part of the invisible Church.

Now we must be careful at this point. One man has quipped, "Being a member of a church doesn't make you a Christian any more than being in a garage makes you a Ford." The late Dr. John Gerstner would often say, "You can be a church member without being a Christian, but you can't be a Christian without being a church member." Was he saying that if you didn't belong to a local church you couldn't be a true Christian no matter what? Was he taking the Romanist position that outside the church there is no salvation? No, I believe I knew that great man well enough to know that he didn't mean that so rigidly. What he meant was that *normally* a person who was a true Christian would be a member of a local Christian church. There might be instances in which the only possibility in a small town was to join a church that was not even Christian itself. And a Christian must not be a member of a non-Christian church, obviously. We are not to do evil that good may come. You do not disobey one of God's commands in order to obey another. A Christian must not be a member of an apostate church or a Buddhist temple just to say that he or she is a member of *some* church. But to be a Christian is to love what God loves, and God loves His Church, which is comprised of His people. The true Christian desires to belong to and affiliate with those people who profess Christ as their Lord and Savior.

It is unfortunate that in our individualistic day and age, few churches have promoted membership. There are many people to whom the idea of local church membership is a novel concept; but it is not novel to God and His Word.

Also, in the Old Testament, God called His people to a specific place, the place where He had chosen for His name to dwell. Nehemiah 1:8–9: "I will gather them from there and will bring them to *the place* where I have chosen to cause My name to dwell." Consider also Psalm 26:8: "O Lord, I love the habitation of Thy house, the place where Thy glory dwells."

You might ask, "Who are the people whom God has called to His house?" The Scripture answers that question in this way: "They are Thy servants and Thy people whom Thou didst redeem by Thy great power and by Thy great hand" (Nehemiah 1:10).

It is certainly true that the New Testament takes for granted the membership of every believer in a local church. We know that, according to Acts 2:42, the people devoted themselves to the apostles' teaching, fellowship, and prayer. Acts 11:25–26 tells us that "they were gathered together *as a church*." And Acts 14:21–23 says that "The apostles taught, and appointed elders for *every church*."

It is noteworthy that the bulk of Paul's letters were written to New Testament churches, not individuals—the church at Philippi, the church at Galatia, the church at Thessalonica, and so on.

Perhaps none of these items on their own would

lead us to an acceptance of the importance of the local church, but together they are substantial and convincing.

To further prove this point, there is much of the Bible which you cannot obey without belonging to a church as a member. For example, we are to respect those over us in the Lord. 1 Thessalonians 5:13: "Appreciate those who have charge over you." How can someone have charge *over* us if we are not in some official way *under* them? We are told by Scripture to obey our leaders. Hebrews 13:17: "Obey your leaders and submit to them, for they keep watch over your souls." The Bible is clear that there are leaders over us, but I know of no leader over the whole Church who is to be obeyed, unless one adopts the Romanist view that the pope is the vicar of Christ and leader over the whole Church, which view I reject, and which view many Romanists reject by virtue of their rejection of papal doctrines and directives in everyday life.

When Paul instructed women to submit themselves to their husbands in everything as unto the Lord, he was enjoining them to place themselves willingly under the head of the house to whom they were married. He did not say that they were to submit to any husband, but to their own. That submission is based upon the official relationship they have to their husband. The same is true in the local church. By virtue of the official relationship of membership, there are leaders we are to obey, and to whom we are to submit. In selecting a local church, as in selecting a husband, we are able to select that person or persons to whom we feel we can submit; but, once the choice is made, submission is no longer optional. It is now God-ordained and God-expected.

Church discipline is given by God, and has long been recognized by the Reformed and evangelical tradition, as one of the marks of a true church. It is commanded and expected by God. But how does a church discipline someone over whom it has no control? On what basis would a non-member accept discipline from a church to which he did not belong? The doctrine and practice of church discipline require church membership. Church discipline is not restricted to excommunication, but without membership it could not be practiced at any level of the disciplinary compendium.

As members of God's universal family, we are to be members of His smaller family unit, the local church. May it please God to bolster the rolls of His local church bodies with active, zealous, passionate members who will take the gospel and give it away.

Jesus shall reign where'er the sun
Does His successive journeys run;
His kingdom spread from shore to shore,
Till moons shall wax and wane no more.

Isaac Watts

Jesus Shall Reign

James White on Authority in the Church

It is the tendency of man to be unbalanced. We never seem content to keep truths in harmony with one another. It is our bent to drift off in one direction or another; and a truth emphasized at the cost of another truth becomes an untruth.

So it is with the Church of Jesus Christ. A multitude of cacophonous voices clamor for our attention, each claiming to represent *the* Church, each saying that they, and they alone, have the special truth that sets *their* church apart from all others. Viewpoints abound as to what the Church is, what her mission is, and what she is to teach and preach. Tremendously unbalanced teachings about the Church are to be found on every hand. Rarely is the Church seen in the light of Scripture; rarely is the balance provided by the Bible allowed its place in our view of the Church. Instead, in broad categories, we see two extremes:

1. The exaltation of the Church to an unbiblical position. Rome and others exalt the Church to a position never given to her in the Scriptures. Rather than recognizing the supremacy of Scripture and the constant need for reformation in the Church, these groups will go so far as to invest the Church with infallibility, ignoring the fact that during her earthly pilgrimage she still struggles and fights, relying upon the Scriptures and the Spirit as her guide. These groups create all sorts of non-biblical offices and trappings which are forced upon the Church. Eventually, in each of these groups, the Church becomes an authority unto herself, and is released from the overriding authority of the God-breathed Word.

Most Protestants are quick to reject such an over-exaltation of the Church. Many evangelicals naturally reject the insertion of unbiblical offices and practices, and see in the papacy an obvious rejection of biblical teaching regarding the Church. Yet, sadly, many of these same evangelicals are satisfied simply to reject the Roman view without ever seriously grappling with their own ecclesiology.

2. *The denigration of the Church to an unbiblical status.* Here we find the greatest ecclesiastical fault of modern American and European evangelical Protestantism: the reshaping of the Christian Church in the form of American consumerism. Allowing society to define what the Church should be has transformed her from the ideal of the New Testament to a mirror image of society itself. The Church is no longer the blessed Bride who is worthy of our service, loyalty, and love. She has become a merchant—selling her wares to the highest bid-

der, cajoling men to enter into her fellowship, begging believers to participate in her work. The term "church shopping" says it all. The Church is a thing marketed to a "target audience," packaged in accordance with polling data, and dressed up so as to attract as many "customers" as possible. It is judged on its size, its wealth, its furnishings, its buildings and its growth rate, just like any other major corporation or business.

It is hardly surprising, then, that the phrase "the authority of the Church" would have a hollow ring to most Protestants standing on the threshold of the third millennium. How can an organization that is based upon my patronage exercise authority over me? How can an assembly that actively sought me out, virtually competing for my participation and giving, in any serious sense exercise authority over my life? I choose the "church of my liking." I can just as easily "unchoose" that assembly, can I not?

How can we balance these two extremes? People who inhabit both ends of the spectrum insist that there is no middle ground, and no way of viewing the Church as both fallible and authoritative, both in need of constant reformation and the "pillar and foundation of the truth" (1 Timothy 3:15). But these are biblical truths, so there must be a way of balancing them and viewing the Church in this way. It

is this harmonious view of Christ's Church that I
desire to present in these pages. I write from two
perspectives: first, as an elder in the Church; second, as one passionately involved in apologetics
and in responding to those who would usurp the
authority of the Scriptures in the Church. I find in
the Apostle Paul a pattern, a template for all who
would labor in service to Christ the King through
His Church, but especially relevant today for all
those who would raise a voice of warning to believers in calling them to a biblical ecclesiology, a
Scriptural view of Christ's Church.

Passion for the Church
Paul's passion for the Church of God flows
through his epistles. The height of his ecclesiology
is captured in a passing remark to his beloved
Timothy:

> But in case I am delayed, I write so that you
> will know how one ought to conduct himself in
> the household of God, which is the church of
> the living God, the pillar and support of the
> truth (1 Timothy 3:15).

The Jewish reader of such a statement is struck
by its import. The "household of God" would remind him of the words of David in 1 Chronicles
29:3, where he speaks of his joy in the "house of

his God" (i.e., the Temple), and other references in
the Scriptures to the "house of God." In the same
way, the reference to the "living God" would bring
up many connections to the God of Israel, like
these words recorded by Moses:

> For who is there of all flesh who has heard the
> voice of the living God speaking from the
> midst of the fire, as we have, and lived?
> (Deuteronomy 5:26).

In the same way, Joshua speaks of Israel's God
as "the living God" (Joshua 3:10), the armies of
Israel are the "armies of the living God" (1 Samuel
17:26), and the Psalmist longed for "the living God"
(Psalm 42:2, cf. Psalm 84:2). The "living God" is
used synonymously for Yahweh, the God of Israel
(Jeremiah 10:10). Paul even chose the same word
for "pillar" here that is used in the Septuagint for
the pillars in the temple in Jerusalem. Any Jew,
familiar with the Scriptures as Timothy was, could
never miss the meaning so plainly communicated
by Paul. When he speaks of the Church as the
"pillar and support of the truth," his doctrine is
based upon the clear recognition of the Church as
the continuing work of God Himself, the very
dwelling place He Himself has chosen. The God of
truth dwells in a people of truth, and those people
make up the Church of Jesus Christ. It is no sur-

prise, then, that the Church is to hold forth the "word of truth, the gospel" (Colossians 1:5). It is her calling, her duty, her function, and it is natural for her to act as the "pillar and support" of the message entrusted to her.

We demonstrate how precious something is to our hearts by the time and energy we invest in it. If someone or something is but rarely upon our hearts and but seldom upon our mind, you can be sure that there is no zeal of love, no deep passion, for that person or thing. Paul confessed to the Corinthians that he experienced the "daily pressure of concern for all the churches" (2 Corinthians 11:28). Every day the welfare of the churches weighed upon Paul's mind, driving him to labor, and to his knees before the living God. And how could he ever forget that he himself had once persecuted what was now the object of his deepest love? Even after years of service to the Church, he could only confess his unworthiness because of his persecution of the Church, which he knew was in reality persecution of his loving Lord:

> For I am the least of the apostles, and not fit to
> be called an apostle, because I persecuted the
> church of God (1 Corinthians 15:9).

But despite his actions, performed before he came face to face with the risen Lord, God was gra-

cious to him, and allowed him not only to be num-
bered among the saints, but to serve Him through
His Church. Paul speaks of himself as a "minister"
of the Church, and one can sense how deeply that
term impressed itself upon his mind:

> Now I rejoice in my sufferings for your sake,
> and in my flesh I do my share on behalf of His
> body, which is the church, in filling up what is
> lacking in Christ's afflictions. Of this church I
> was made a minister according to the steward-
> ship from God bestowed on me for your bene-
> fit, so that I might fully carry out the preach-
> ing of the word of God, that is, the mystery
> which has been hidden from the past ages and
> generations, but has now been manifested to
> His saints, to whom God willed to make known
> what is the riches of the glory of this mystery
> among the Gentiles, which is Christ in you,
> the hope of glory (Colossians 1:24–27).

The apostle showed his deep love and concern
by making provision for the churches. He did so
not only through his epistles, but through the appointment of godly elders within the congregations
(Acts 14:23; 1 Timothy 5:17; Titus 1:5). Indeed, so
high is the New Testament's view of this calling
that Luke could speak of the "apostles and elders"
at Jerusalem (Acts 15:2, 16:4). Such a conjunction
of terms speaks directly to Paul's view of the elder-

ship. Peter likewise saw in the office of elder a great provision for the Church, patterned after the caring and loving Chief Shepherd Himself:

> Therefore, I exhort the elders among you, as your fellow elder and witness of the sufferings of Christ, and a partaker also of the glory that is to be revealed, to shepherd the flock of God among you, exercising oversight not under compulsion, but voluntarily, according to the will of God; and not for sordid gain, but with eagerness; nor yet as lording it over those allotted to your charge, but proving to be examples to the flock. And when the Chief Shepherd appears, you will receive the unfading crown of glory (1 Peter 5:1–4).

But by far the most exalted language flows from the apostle's pen when he writes to the Ephesians about the "unfathomable riches" of Christ, the great mystery of the Church. Any believer must work hard to even attempt to grasp the length and breadth of Paul's description of the Church. He refers to the Church as "His [Christ's] body," with Christ at its head, "the fullness of Him who fills all in all" (Ephesians 1:22–23).[1]   Here the resurrected

---

[1] Interpretations differ on the meaning of "the fullness of Him who fills all in all." Calvin writes: "This is the highest honor of the Church, that, until He is united to us, the Son

Lord, who stands at the right hand of the Majesty on High, deigns to have the Church identified as His body. The relationship between Christ and His Church is undeniably intimate and personal. Anyone who would love the Lord, then, must naturally love His Church as well, for it is His "body." But the apostle has only just begun:

> To me, the very least of all saints, this grace was given, to preach to the Gentiles the un-

---

of God reckons Himself in some measure imperfect. What consolation is it for us to learn, that, not until we are along with Him, does He possess all his parts, or wish to be regarded as complete!" (John Calvin, *Commentary on Ephesians*, Calvin Collection CD-ROM, 1998). He quickly adds, however, that the phrase "who fills all in all" is added "to guard against the supposition that any real defect would exist in Christ, if He were separated from us. His wish to be filled, and, in some respects, made perfect in us, arises from no want or necessity; for all that is good in ourselves, or in any of the creatures, is the gift of His hand; and His goodness appears the more remarkably in raising us out of nothing, that He, in like manner, may dwell and live in us." The final phrase from Calvin leads to the majority understanding of the passage, that it is Christ who fills His Church.

The KJV and NKJV read "in the church by Christ Jesus" rather than "in the church and in Christ Jesus," following the *Textus Receptus* reading. Yet the earliest manuscripts of Ephesians, and all the earliest uncial texts, read as the NASB.

> fathomable riches of Christ, and to bring to
> light what is the administration of the mystery
> which for ages has been hidden in God who
> created all things; so that the manifold wisdom
> of God might now be made known through the
> church to the rulers and the authorities in the
> heavenly places (Ephesians 3:8–10).

Paul, a minister of the Church, was commissioned to do what each and every minister in her service must do: "preach the unfathomable riches of Christ." He likewise "brought to light" the very plan of God which was hidden for ages in the Creator Himself. And how is this "manifold wisdom of God" made known to the "rulers and the authorities in the heavenly places"? What mechanism has God chosen to reveal His great wisdom and power? The Church. Can we imagine a higher doctrine than this? The very wisdom of God being revealed through Christ's Church? The Church as a demonstration of God's wisdom? Do not such descriptions thrill the heart of the churchman? Yet how many in our day, when thinking of the Church, think in a truly apostolic fashion? If the Church reveals God's wisdom (through the proclamation of His truth, the gospel), how can anyone suggest that she needs to be "updated," or that we should employ "marketing strategies" to promote her work? When we define the Church by her mission (the revelation of God's wisdom in Christ), all the man-centered and man-oriented "programs" that have become all the rage in the Church are seen to be utterly incompatible with the high privilege and calling of Christ's bride, the Church!

The Church is a glorious place, according to Paul. That is, he teaches that God is glorified in the Church:

> to Him be the glory in the church and in Christ Jesus to all generations forever and ever. Amen (Ephesians 3:21).

This tremendous doxology offers praise to God the Father by asserting that He will be glorified eternally in the Church and in Christ Jesus. It is not as if these are two different ways of God being glorified, as if the Church can be viewed separately from Christ. Christ dwells within His Church; hence any glorification of the Father that takes place in the Church does so in Christ.

But these previous descriptions are only the prelude to the pinnacle of Paul's thought, expressed in the analogy of the marriage relationship with that of Christ and His Church. These words are familiar to most Christians, yet we cannot avoid Paul's words that he speaks of a "great mystery" (5:32), and therefore cannot ever think that we have exhausted the depth of the revelation made here:

> For the husband is the head of the wife, as
> Christ also is the head of the church, He
> Himself being the Savior of the body. But as
> the church is subject to Christ, so also the
> wives ought to be to their husbands in every-
> thing. Husbands, love your wives, just as
> Christ also loved the church and gave Himself
> up for her, so that He might sanctify her,
> having cleansed her by the washing of water
> with the word, that He might present to
> Himself the church in all her glory, having no
> spot or wrinkle or any such thing; but that
> she would be holy and blameless (Ephesians
> 5:23–27).

Christ is the Head of the Church, the Savior of
the body. The Church is subject to Christ, loved by
Christ, sanctified by Christ, cleansed by Christ, and
all so that He can present her to Himself glorious,
without spot or wrinkle. The Church will be made
holy and blameless by the almighty Savior; it is His
purpose, His task, and He cannot possibly fail to
accomplish His goal.

The holy and blameless Church—such exalted
language has provided the basis for those who
have sought to invest the Church of Christ with attributes of perfection during her earthly sojourn.
And surely if these were the only words of the apostle regarding the Church, we could understand
such a conclusion. But they are not. Balanced exe-

gesis requires us to look at all the apostle said. We must hold in one hand the highest view of the Church, His body, and hold her precious in our sight. But we must likewise hear the warnings the apostle provides regarding false teachers and the struggles the Church will face through the ages. We must take seriously the provision the apostle provides for the Church, and what it means that she must face struggle and hardship here on earth before she enters into her final rest in glory. We must balance the passages that speak of the need for correction, constant vigilance, and the dangers that surround her on her pilgrimage. To some of these passages we now turn.

A Warning and a Provision

Final words are important words. When we gather at the bedside of a loved one who is about to depart this world, we know that what is going to be said carries the greatest importance. We all wish to have the opportunity to say our final goodbyes and make those final statements by which we desire to be remembered.

Twice in Scripture we have the opportunity of hearing final words on the part of the Apostle Paul. The first instance comes as he journeys to Jerusalem, knowing full well that imprisonment awaits him there. He calls for the elders of the

church at Ephesus to meet him (Acts 20:17–38).
The church obviously held a special place in his
heart, for he had spent a great deal of time ministering there. His words are filled with strong emo-
tion. What does he say to these beloved men at this
momentous time? Does he focus upon himself, his
accomplishments, his trials and troubles? No,
rather he focuses upon the Church, the body of
Christ he served with his entire being. He exhorts
the elders to shepherd the flock of God and watch
out for false teachers within the fellowship, and he
commends them to God and the word of His grace
(Acts 20:32).

In the same fashion, as Paul faced the end of
his life under Roman arrest years later, he wrote to
his beloved son in the faith, Timothy. The years of
imprisonment and trial had not changed the focus
of the great apostle. He had not become bitter and
focused upon his trials and difficulties. The apple
of his eye remained the same: glorifying His Lord
through service to the Lord's Church. Just as he
had warned the Ephesian elders of what lay ahead
for them, so too he warns Timothy, and provides
him with all that he needs to continue his ministry
in the face of trials and difficulties (2 Timothy 3:
1–17). I will use these two passages to provide the
proper balance to the description of the Church
provided by Paul, not in the sense that his exalted

language now requires some kind of correction, but in the sense that the same apostle recognized the "now and not yet" of the Church's glory, just as he did in reference to the believer. While he could speak of the believer as "seated in the heavenly places" (Ephesians 2:6), he could also say, "Test yourselves" (2 Corinthians 13:5), and "Be alert and sober" (1 Thessalonians 5:6). Both are part and parcel of our reality as believers, and, in the same way, the Church experiences both elements in her earthly sojourn.

Acts 20:17–38 provides one of the most gripping scenes in all of Luke's history. Paul calls for the elders at Ephesus, gathers together with them, and (with an intensity matched only in his letters to Timothy) exhorts them in the strongest terms to pursue the calling of God upon their lives. He first speaks of how he had fulfilled the ministry given to him by his Lord Jesus Christ "to testify solemnly of the gospel of the grace of God" (Acts 20:24), and how they will never see his face again. Then he gives them an exhortation and a warning:

> Be on guard for yourselves and for all the flock, among which the Holy Spirit has made you overseers, to shepherd the church of God which He purchased with His own blood. I know that after my departure savage wolves will come in among you, not sparing the flock;

> and from among your own selves men will
> arise, speaking perverse things, to draw away
> the disciples after them. Therefore be on the
> alert, remembering that night and day for a
> period of three years I did not cease to admon-
> ish each one with tears (Acts 20:28–31).

The apostle expresses a deep love and concern
for the "flock" which is the "church of God." He
exhorts the elders to be diligent in their duty as
shepherds of the precious flock of God which was
purchased at the cost of the very blood of the Son
of God. The elders are to look to themselves, for
Satan attempts to disrupt the Church by undermin-
ing her leaders. Indeed, Paul says it is from among
the elders that false teachers will arise. Therefore,
they must be diligent. They must also look carefully after the flock. As shepherds, they must have a
heart for their task, a love for those placed under
their care. The great cost of the flock shows how
precious in the sight of God is the Church, and the
mention of the Holy Spirit's role in placing them in
their position shows the intimate relationship between the Lord and His Church. These elders are to
undertake their ministry with full assurance that
their task is divine, for they have been placed in
their position not by men, but by the Holy Spirit.
He equips men with the necessary gifts for their
work in the Church, and by divine wisdom places

them exactly where He sovereignly chooses.

Constant vigilance and diligence in the work of shepherding the flock are necessary because of what lies ahead for the fledgling Church. Paul does not merely suggest that there are difficult times ahead; he boldly asserts that he knows that after his departure "savage wolves" will enter into the Church. And his prediction is all the more troubling for its specificity: he is not merely speaking of false teachers attacking the fellowship from without, but these false teachers will arise from within the eldership itself. These ravenous animals, by nature the enemies of the sheep of the flock, will specifically seek to feed off the flock, drawing disciples after themselves even while speaking "perverse things." The term can mean "perverse" in the sense of "obviously twisted," or it can have a less strident meaning and refer to something bent or misshapen. Many false doctrines are obviously "perverse" in that they blatantly deny Christian truth (Jehovah's Witnesses denying the deity of Christ and the resurrection, or Mormons teaching that God was once a man). But others are just "bent," maintaining the appearance of truth while being altered just enough to allow the "ravenous wolf" to draw disciples after himself.

We dare not miss the weight of the apostle's warning. God has not made the Church immune to such men. There is no promise that as soon as a false teacher arises in the congregation, God will strike that person dumb, or cause him to glow a strange color so that all will see. While at least once God struck a false teacher blind (Acts 13:9–12), such is not the normal pattern. The Church in her everyday walk will have to struggle against false teaching and false teachers, and it is plain that those who trouble the Church will claim allegiance to her. From the world's perspective, just as it was in the days of the apostles, it will be Christian versus Christian as well as Christian versus unbeliever. The labels worn by the various sides will not, in and of themselves, truly tell the story. Apostates were a constant irritant to the apostolic ministry, and there is nothing in Scripture that warrants a belief that such difficulties would end when the apostles completed their ministry. Just the opposite is true.

This is why the elders must actively shepherd the flock of God, for dangers abound. Paul goes on to exhort them, in light of the approaching wolves, to "be on the alert," which speaks of an ongoing, constant state of vigilance, the price of truth for the Church. Just as he had worked so hard among them, so too they must now bend their backs to the task ahead.

Paul warns the Church and exhorts the elders,

but upon what basis is the battle to be waged? What provisions does he make for the difficulties he prophesies? It is just here that we touch upon the very marrow of the appeal of authoritarian systems and those religious systems that make of the Church something other than her Founder intended. The cry is so often heard, "There is so much confusion; there are so many different views! We need an infallible authority to define the truth for us, and the Bible just isn't enough to do it! Follow the successors of Peter!" Surely, if there were ever a time for Paul to direct the leaders of the Church to obedience to Peter, or Peter's successors, or any other such external, extra-biblical source of authority, it would be in the 32nd verse of the twentieth chapter of Acts. Surely, when you warn someone of impending danger, you make provision for handling the problem! When a military commander says, "An attack is imminent," it is expected that his next orders will provide for a defense against the attack. When the boss is going out of town, he leaves his subordinates with contingency plans to handle emergencies. When parents leave a teenager in charge while they go on an errand, they make provision for handling problems as they arise. Surely the apostle would be no less caring and no less concerned!

So what provision does Paul provide to the

Church in the face of imminent assault by false
teachers disguised as Christian leaders? His words
are succinct and telling (Acts 20:32):

> And now I commend you to God and to the
> word of His grace, which is able to build you
> up and to give you the inheritance among all
> those who are sanctified.

Paul literally "delivers over" or "entrusts" (the
same term used by the Lord Jesus when, in Luke
23:46, He cried out, "Father, into Your hands I
commit My spirit") the Church and her elders into
the hands of God Himself and the word of His
grace. Here is provision unparalleled, security un-
surpassed. Their security and defense is not found
in external structures, but in the internal fact of
God's sovereignty and power, His love for the
Church, and the truth that ever abides in her
(2 John 2). The Church's strength is the same as
the individual believer's: "for when I am weak, then
I am strong" (2 Corinthians 12:10). The Church's
strength is in fidelity to her Lord and in faithfulness to His word of grace. It is this foolishness (for
so the worldly mind must call it) that causes so
many to stumble. The strength and capacity are
found in God and His gospel, not in the Church,
and not in those who make up the Church. Just as
the bride looks to her husband for protection, so

the Bride looks to the Bridegroom, never to herself. She glories in her weakness, and in His strength.

How does the Church know the word of His grace, the message of the cross? From the God-breathed Scriptures. This is exactly what Paul would say years later, after many more trials, many more difficulties had flowed through his life. None of these changed his singular focus upon the truly divine provision for the Church. Here are his words:

> Indeed, all who desire to live godly in Christ Jesus will be persecuted. But evil men and impostors will proceed from bad to worse, deceiving and being deceived. You, however, continue in the things you have learned and become convinced of, knowing from whom you have learned them, and that from childhood you have known the sacred writings which are able to give you the wisdom that leads to salvation through faith which is in Christ Jesus. All Scripture is inspired by God and profitable for teaching, for reproof, for correction, and for training in righteousness; so that the man of God may be adequate, equipped for every good work (2 Timothy 3:12–17).

The same pattern emerges here in Paul's deeply-felt farewell message to Timothy as is found in his goodbye to the elders at Ephesus: warning, exhortation, and provision. The warning remains the same: deceivers will grow worse; deception and falsehood remain the constant foe. But Timothy is not to despair in the face of these trials, but is exhorted to remain faithful and consistent. And to what source is he directed by his mentor? Just as Paul had directed the Ephesian elders to God and His word of grace, so Timothy is told that all he needs in order to be a man of God and to pursue his ministry of teaching in the Church will be found in that which is "inspired" or "God-breathed," the Scriptures. They are sufficient to equip him thoroughly for every good work. And one of the works mentioned is "correcting," something the man of God must do in the Church (2 Timothy 2:24–26).

The Balance Maintained

The same apostle spoke often of rebuking, exhorting, and disciplining, all in the context of the Church. He warned of false teachers arising within the Church, and exhorted the Church's leaders to constant vigilance in defense of the truth. Yet, at times, within the same epistle, he spoke of the Church as glorious, spotless, the very pillar and foundation of the truth, the Church of the living God. We err grievously if we adopt any one element of the divine truth about the Church to the detriment of the other. The one leads inexorably to papalism and absolutism. But the other is just as dangerous, just as deadly. It leads to a disrespect for the Church, and a denigration of her authority to act as the pillar and foundation of the truth, the divine means God has ordained to demonstrate His wisdom to the world. The one makes believers slaves to an unyielding and uncorrectable master; the other makes the Church the slave to a finicky, particular constituency always looking for something new, looking to be made to "feel good." Neither will do.

He who loves Christ will love His body, the Church. He who seeks to obey Christ will have respect for the divine institution of the Church and those whom the Spirit places within that body to teach, exhort, and rebuke. The balanced presentation the Bible makes of the Church leaves no room for papalism, nor for the modern consumer-oriented ecclesiology of so much of evangelicalism. Instead, the Word of God presents to us a Church that is the household of the living God, His flock, indwelt by Him, filled by Him, loved by Him, led by men appointed by the Holy Spirit as shepherds, leading the flock in eager and zealous service of the Lord Christ, all leading to the glory of God.

Rescue the perishing, care for the dying,
Snatch them in pity from sin and the grave;
Weep o'er the erring one, lift up the fallen,
Tell them of Jesus, the mighty to save.

Fanny J. Crosby

Weep O'er the Erring One, Lift Up the Fallen

John H. Armstrong on Church Discipline

There can be little doubt about it. The church in North America is in serious trouble. Many of her failings are above the surface, in plain view for most of us who love her to see. She also has great need of much that we might think of as being below the surface. These needs are not so obvious. They run, however, like a great subterranean river, impacting everything the church does in the open. These particular needs call us to serious, concentrated effort if we are to pursue true reformation. The largest underground river of all is what I would call "true and vital holiness." Everywhere one looks there is abundant evidence that the church has lost its way in terms of biblical, personal, Christ-like holiness. Yes, the river of holiness runs deep within the lives of those who love God, those who are called according to His purpose. But it must also be encouraged, and if encouraged it must find public expression in the corporate body, the visible church.

As important as good theology is—and there really is no substitute for doctrinal soundness in any

131

church—even sound theology will not cause the
church to be a powerful instrument in the hands of
the living God. Only when the church believes correctly, confesses the truth faithfully, *and* lives a life
of Christ-centered holiness will she become a
mighty instrument in the hands of God.

In Revelation 3 our Lord spoke from heaven to
the first-century church in Laodicea. His counsel
was direct and searching. Can there really be serious doubt that His words apply *specifically* to the
modern church in North America? The church, in
our time, also claims to be rich in every way, to
have acquired great wealth, and to need almost
nothing. Yet our Lord's rebuke corrects our age
when He says, "But you do not realize that you are
wretched, pitiful, poor, blind and naked" (3:17).

The Lord Jesus counsels us to get three things
from Him. First is "gold, refined in the fire, so you
can become rich." This wealthy church in ancient
Asia Minor was, in reality, very poor with God.
Second, Jesus counsels this church to get "white
clothes to wear, so you can cover . . . shameful
nakedness." This church, so much like the church
in North America at the end of this millennium,
was morally and ethically bankrupt. It claimed so
much, but when faced with a holy, enthroned, and
sovereign Christ, it had so little to offer. Finally,
Jesus counsels this church to get "salve to put on

[their] eyes, so you can see" (Revelation 3:18). These people thought that they could see things so clearly, but their love of the world had actually blinded them to the glories of the gospel.

The simple fact is this: whenever the church is genuinely renewed her visible life, expressed in community, will be renewed in true holiness. This is especially true with regard to the *practice* of corporate holiness, which will inevitably result in the recovery of church discipline.

Two Types of Discipline

In order to understand church discipline at all, we must recognize that there are two types of church discipline: formative and corrective. Most of us, when we hear the words "church discipline," immediately think of one thing—putting people out of the church. This response is most unfortunate. First-century disciples, as well as our evangelical forefathers, did not think in this manner. Note this excellent expression of the matter, from an evangelical writer of the last century:

> We may say of a Christian church, that it is well-disciplined, not when perpetually engaged in efforts to reclaim offenders, but when there are few offenders to be reclaimed. That notion of church discipline, which regards it as pertaining entirely, or chiefly, to the settlement of

difficulties, and the treatment of cases of delinquency, is altogether too limited. It takes a far
wider range. It embraces such a judicious administration of the laws of Christ in His visible
kingdom, and such training of His subjects to
habits of active obedience, that difficulties and
delinquencies shall scarcely be known. Like
military and family discipline, it includes a
formative, as well as a corrective, or reforma-
tive process. . . . It implies, in short, nothing
less than a full and faithful application of those
scriptural rules and principles, which were
designed to preserve the order of the
churches, to promote the purity, harmony,
and useful efficiency of their faithful members,
and to separate the incorrigibly unfaithful
from their communion and fellowship.[1]

So it is appropriate to think of church discipline
in these two senses, not simply as excommunication from the privileges of church fellowship.

Love or Obedience?
Our generation tends to recoil at the mention of
excluding anyone from the church. This reaction
actually begins with the failure to understand the

---

[1] Warham Walker, *Church Discipline: An Exposition of the
Scripture Doctrine of Church Order and Government*
(Rochester, N.Y.: Backus Book Publishers, 1981 reprint of
1844 edition), p. 4.

whole concept of *formative* discipline. We seem to think love is letting people do whatever they wish, regardless of the consequences. We have come to think of love as the exact opposite of discipline. After all, what business is it of ours to judge someone else?

I was reminded of this deeply ingrained pattern of thought while watching the historic Congressional impeachment proceedings against President Bill Clinton. As one impassioned speaker after another rose to argue against possible impeachment, the most common thread in the entire argument could be heard in the oft-quoted words of Jesus: "Judge not lest you be judged." I feel sure this text must now be the best-known verse in all the Bible! I also feel sure that it is also the least-understood verse in all the Bible. But serious Christians ought to know better, or so you would think. Could it be that our long decline from concern for personal holiness has brought us to the place where even the words of our Lord are subject to such gross perversion, both in the world and in the church?

But does this statement of Jesus really mean we should never exercise church discipline, no matter how badly the offender has sinned? The most obvious problem with this approach is that it fails to take into account the very basis of New Testament church life. The congregation of a well-ordered,

scriptural church must be made up of those who
live orderly lives in conformity with the gospel, both
in their confession of faith and in their lifestyle. If
this problem is to be adequately addressed, we
must become more intentional and careful in accepting new members into our churches. And we
must admonish and correct members as long as
they are under the care of our particular church.

It was, after all, Christ Himself who instituted
church discipline (cf. Matthew 18:15–20); and upon
more careful reading it is apparent that the New
Testament epistles repeatedly reaffirm its importance. Dare we ignore this subject, so plainly taught
in God's Word, and then expect God to bless us?
We must obey Christ, and not the dictates of cul-
tural "love." If we surrender to the modern concept
we will continue to practice a love that gives little
or no place to discipline, whether in the home, the
school, or the larger society. (This is one of the
more disconcerting aspects of high public approval
ratings for a President who has plainly confessed
serious misconduct! Even more disconcerting, in
my opinion, is the continued support this same
President receives from evangelical leaders who act
as if a moment of public humiliation is sufficient
for the complete restoration of character and personal responsibility.)

But how did we get to this point? How could the

church profess so strongly its allegiance to Christ while at the same time making so little of the matter of church discipline?

> Put simply, the abandonment of church discipline is linked to American Christianity's creeping accommodation to American culture. As the twentieth century began, this accommodation became increasingly evident as the church acquiesced to a culture of moral individualism.[2]

Look for the Fruit of Repentance

Formative discipline entails all the means that Scripture gives us for building a church of spiritually healthful and genuinely holy people. The very best system of corrective church discipline cannot be applied to people who are not ready for it. Many a modern pastor has found this out the hard way by introducing the practice of corrective discipline to a congregation that had little understanding of the church, and even less of "tough love," biblically defined.

Obviously no human can look into the heart of

---

2 R. Albert Mohler, Jr., ["The Missing Mark"] in *The Compromised Church*, ed. John H. Armstrong (Wheaton, Ill.: Crossway, 1998), 172. This brilliant and clear essay should be consulted for further helpful and thoughtful reflection upon the subject of church discipline in our time.

prospective members and determine finally and objectively who is regenerate and who is not. Faithful leaders can, however, look for credible evidences of sound confession. They can ask: "Is the fruit of genuine repentance present in this person's life? How do we know?"

As a pastor, when I engaged in the interview of new members, I tried to determine the answer to at least three questions in this regard: (1) Does this person confess sin personally and give evidence of hating and forsaking it? (2) Is there evidence of a cheerful performance of the duties described in Scripture? (3) Does this person demonstrate contrition and biblical humility of spirit? Is there at least some measure of brokenness?

But what if we discover weakness in the prospective member? This is no reason for exclusion. Instead we are to receive weaker believers and "bear with" their failings (cf. Romans 15:1–2). But if we see evidence that the confession is unsound, this is a different matter. We have a clear responsibility to wait, or even to ultimately refuse the request for membership.

A well-ordered gospel church begins to restore discipline by first seeking to determine if the membership has understood and savingly embraced the gospel.

Instructing the Church in Godliness

But what about members who are already in the flock and were not taught properly *before* they were received? And what about the human tendency to lose our way and to forget what we once knew?

In addition to adhering to scriptural principles regarding the reception of new members, we must continually instruct our congregations. The writer of Hebrews was rightly concerned about his readers. Some of them should by this time, he reasoned, be teachers themselves. Yet, he argues, they still needed to be taught some of the most basic principles of God's Word all over again (cf. 5:12). They still were unable to distinguish between good and evil. What a sad picture of many in the church. Even if the seeds of true faith and genuine repentance are found, there will still be the desperate need to grow up, even in some of the most basic truths. We who lead must never stop training our flocks in godliness.

Today, sadly, we emphasize meeting "felt needs." Very little practical instruction in godly living comes from this environment. How many churches reason that their youth, for example, need lots of fun activities and short, relevant Bible lessons, or simple moral lessons? Such was not the case in generations past when children were taught catechisms and doctrinal statements at tender ages.

In light of the laid-back way we teach and preach today, Paul's description of his own ministry is quite startling: "We proclaim Him, admonishing and teaching everyone with all wisdom, so that we may present everyone perfect in Christ. To this end I labor, struggling with all His energy, which so powerfully works in me" (Colossians 1:28–29).

For pastors and elders the task is clear: to "struggle." But why? In order that our flocks will be well taught and that our people will be "perfected" (matured) in Christ. But why is this so vital? If we do not struggle, the people may fall into serious sin and be unable to distinguish that which is truly good from that which is evil and sinful.

Formative discipline will use several measures to bring the people of God to maturity:

1. *Faithful, systematic, pastoral instruction.* Pastors have been given by God, says the apostle, to prepare His people for "works of service, so that the body of Christ may be built up until we all reach unity in the faith and in the knowledge of the Son of God and become mature, attaining to the whole measure of the fullness of Christ" (Ephesians 4:12–13).

2. *A higher level of personal piety and biblical knowledge among chosen leaders.* In light of 1 Timothy 3:1–13 and Titus 1:6–9, how can we ever apply

these principles of discipline to the church if our leaders are not "above reproach"?

3. *Leaders who act more as shepherds and less as business executives.* Pastors are responsible for the watchful care and oversight of the flock. "Preach the Word; be prepared in season and out of season; correct, rebuke and encourage—with great patience and careful instruction" (2 Timothy 4:2).

4. *Cultivation of mutual care and counsel among the flock.* To the Colossians, Paul wrote: "Let the word of Christ dwell in you richly as you teach and admonish one another with all wisdom" (3:16). We need to restudy the various "one anothers" of the New Testament and make room for them in our church life.

5. *Building a loyalty to the basic meetings of our assemblies* (Hebrews 10:25). For too many, the church is no longer a community of faithful followers of Christ, but rather a one-hour-per-week event. We see the church not as a called-out people on mission for their Master, but as a retail store that waits on us when we "need" it to help us.

The Final Court of Appeal

All of this responsibility has been given directly to the church by our Lord. Not only does Jesus make it perfectly clear that the church is the final court in matters of ecclesiastical discipline (cf.

Matthew 18:15–20), but so does the Apostle Paul. In 1 Corinthians 5 it is very clear that it was the business of the gathered church to "put out" of its fellowship the immoral man in question (5:2). Paul asks, "What business is it of mine to judge those outside the church? Are you [plural] not to judge those inside [i.e., within the fellowship of your own church]?" (5:12). He then commands them very clearly: "Expel the wicked man from among you [plural, i.e., from your congregation]."

Two things are apparent here: this man's exclusion was commanded by the apostle, but the action was to be taken only after an orderly, deliberate and solemn decision made by the assembly in Corinth. Please observe: though elders and deacons may, and do, serve as spiritual caregivers and leaders in the disciplinary process, *ultimately* it is the church that must act, even if upon the counsel and recommendation of its leadership. In 2 Corinthians 2:6 Paul makes this point abundantly clear when he refers to this action of discipline as "the punishment inflicted on him by the majority." And the decision of this assembly, if a correct and biblical one, is ratified in heaven (cf. Matthew 18:18). All of this makes the action of the congregation doubly serious. No member of the church can "wash his hands" of these matters if they are properly dealt with according to the Scripture. J. Robertson

McQuilkin understood this point when he wrote several decades ago:

> It is significant that the New Testament emphasis on both unity and purity has to do with the local congregation. In contrast, most of the emphasis in the twentieth century, whether on unity or on purity, is on larger interchurch or interdenominational relationships. But it is at the level of the local congregation that both unity or purity is most visible. And this is where the battle for unity or purity must be won or lost.[3]

The local congregation is also where unity and purity are most difficult to achieve and maintain.

Why Not Simply Look the Other Way?

When discipline is called for, and the church does not act in accordance with the Word of God, that congregation stands under the judgment of God! Listen again to wise counsel from the previous century:

> It is impossible that a church in which corrective discipline is neglected should be a prosperous church. Aside from the forfeiture of the

---

[3] J. Robertson McQuilkin, *Christianity Today*, March 29, 1974.

divine favor, which is incurred by such neglect, and which must prove fatal to all true
prosperity, the allowance of sin, uncensured,
in church members has a natural tendency to
disastrous results.

A pernicious and rapidly corrupting example
is thereby introduced into the body. If one
member may transgress, unquestioned and
uncondemned, so may another, and another;
and the evil will extend itself, until the entire
church is pervaded. "A little leaven leaveneth
the whole lump."

A little root of bitterness, if it be suffered to
grow and spread, will defile many. A slight
gangrenous affection [sic], if its progress be
not stayed, will speedily pass through the
whole body, prostrating its energies, and
turning its comeliness into corruption. In like
manner, offenses committed by church members, if tolerated, "will increase unto more ungodliness" (1 Cor. 5:6; Heb. 12:15; 2 Tim. 2:16–
17).[4]

It never ceases to amaze me how local churches
will pursue policies and practices that virtually
preclude their own corrective discipline. We cannot
"look the other way" when erring children fall. We
must lovingly discipline them. Can the same be

---

[4] Walker, *Church Discipline,* pp. 76–77.

any less true of the family of Christ gathered together in His church?

How long can a church experience the manifest
presence of Christ in its midst if it refuses His direct counsel? Because we do not see a physical
Christ leaving most of our churches, we assume
that He is still with us, manifesting His power and
blessing, no matter what we have done to grieve
Him. This, it seems to me, is precisely why true revivals have often come at precisely the moment
when a church restores the mandated discipline of
the New Testament.[5]

Keep the Proper Objective in Mind

What should be the church's objective in practicing corrective discipline? If members of the
church are sinning, will not be restored, and refuse
to listen to biblical counsel, it is the church's duty
to discipline as our Lord commands. But if we
carry out discipline in false zeal, we may well carry
out the right actions without the grand objects of

---

[5] In studying the great moves of God in revival I have noted
this fact time after time. Churches, as we shall later see, often
begin to restore the mark of church discipline and then
discover the Spirit powerfully present with them, touching
the lives of many, restoring believers who have fallen, and
adding a great harvest of new converts to the local congregations of a particular area.

God's will before us, thus erring seriously in what we actually do. This is so important that we need to consider it briefly.

It is imperative that we have clear in our thinking what these correct objects are. I believe that there are five objectives in church discipline that need to be kept before us at all times.

1. *To preserve the church's purity and to avoid profaning the Holy Supper of our Lord Jesus Christ.* In this vein, ponder afresh 1 Corinthians 5:6–8 and 11:27. In both instances Paul reasons that bad conduct has serious consequences for the whole family.

2. *To vindicate the honor and integrity of Christ.* Paul wrote to the Corinthians about the case of an incestuous member in their midst to "see if you would stand the test and be obedient to everything" (2 Corinthians 2:9). If we fail to honor the glorious name of Christ by neglecting our responsibility to discipline fallen brothers and sisters, then the world's respect for us will lessen as well. Over the long run, the church's members will lose confidence in her. This will often occur in ways that are not seen, at least initially. When ethical behavior fails to honor God, both His name and teaching are "slandered" (1 Timothy 6:1), and the way of truth is brought "into disrepute" (2 Peter 2:2).

3. *To deter others from serious sin.* One of the obvious benefits of any type of discipline is that it acts

as a deterrent. Paul says, regarding the elders who protect the flock: "Those who sin are to be rebuked publicly, so that the others may take warning" (1 Timothy 5:20).

The "Teacher" in Ecclesiastes observes, "When the sentence for a crime is not quickly carried out, the hearts of the people are filled with schemes to do wrong" (Ecclesiastes 8:11).

4. *To keep God from having to set Himself against the local church.* This objective has in mind Revelation 2:14–15. In regard to the church at Pergamum, Jesus says, "I have a few things against you." For the church at Thyatira, He also says, "Nevertheless, I have this against you." Personally, I have no doubt that if many churches in North America, at the end of this century, were to hear from Christ directly, these might well be the first words spoken by Him.

5. *To bring about the repentance of the offender and spiritual reclamation.* On the human side, our goal is always to "gain" our brother or sister. We do not discipline to repel the offender, but rather to teach and restore to moral soundness.

"If your brother sins against you," says Jesus, "go and show him his fault, just between the two of you. If he listens to you, you have won your brother over" (Matthew 18:15). That is, you have helped to *restore* him spiritually. All admonition must be

given with this end in view. The man referred to in
1 Corinthians 5:5 is disciplined "so that the sinful
nature [flesh] may be destroyed and his spirit
saved on the day of the Lord."[6]

The Essential Priority

By far the overriding concern in the practice of
church discipline must always be the glory of God!
The Holy One of heaven and earth must be hon-
ored, and His word must be obeyed. The cry of the
redeemed in heaven must more frequently become
the cry of the redeemed on earth: "To Him who sits
on the throne and to the Lamb be praise and honor
and glory and power, forever and ever" (Revelation
5:13).

Would that all churches would begin to consider this important matter of church discipline at
this time. Only here will we find the proper motiva-
tion for reforming the church.

Two Extremes To Be Avoided

But in actually coming to restore church discipline, nothing is perhaps more important than
seeking to maintain a right spirit within the church

---

6 Walker, *Church Discipline,* pp. 82–89. These reasons are
frequently cited by many older writers and provide an
adequate summation of the essential concerns of true
discipline.

family. Here, as everywhere, we must guard against extremes. The great English Baptist theologian-minister Andrew Fuller (1754–1815) offered wise counsel in regard to the various extremes that may enter into the church when discipline is carried out. Fuller wrote:

> There are two errors in particular into which individuals have frequently fallen in these matters. One is a harsh and unfeeling conduct towards the offender, tending only to provoke his resentment, or to drive him to despair; the other is that of siding with him, apologizing for him, and carrying it so familiarly towards him in private as to induce him to think others who reprove him his enemies.
>
> Beware, brethren, of both of these extremes, which, instead of assisting us in our work, would be doing the utmost to counteract us. We may also as well abandon discipline as not to act in concert.
>
> It was on this principle that the apostle enjoined it on the Corinthians "not to keep company, if any man that is called a brother be a fornicator, or covetous, or an idolater, or a railer, or a drunkard, or an extortioner; with such a one, not to eat."[7]

---

[7] Andrew Fuller, *The Complete Works of the Rev. Andrew*

Love

Surely, in disciplining church members, a spirit of love, real love which results in genuine kindness and selfless concern, should characterize *all* who are involved. We must always be "quick to listen, slow to speak and slow to become angry" (James 1:19). Continually we must remind ourselves of the great truths taught by the apostle who exhorted the Corinthians regarding the character of true love:

> Love is patient, love is kind. It does not envy, it does not boast, it is not proud. It is not rude, it is not self-seeking, it is not easily angered, it keeps no record of wrongs. Love does not delight in evil but rejoices with the truth. It always protects, always trusts, always hopes, always perseveres (1 Corinthians 13:4–7).

The law of Christ concerning corrective church discipline is really rather simple. It allows no place for spiritual domination or personal revenge. This is not a weapon to be used, but a tearful appeal to be faithfully made.

Fuller, ed. Joseph Belcher (Harrisonburg, Va.: Sprinkle Publications, 1988, II:463.

Do We Have a Universal Principle for This Practice?

The essential text for the practice of church discipline is clearly Matthew 18:15–20. The church has long understood the text as the place where the binding will of our Lord, regarding corrective discipline, is to be discovered. (Only here and in Matthew 16:18 does our Lord ever speak explicitly of the church.)

> If your brother sins against you, go and show him his fault, just between the two of you. If he listens to you, you have won your brother over. But if he will not listen, take one or two others along, so that "every matter may be established by the testimony of two or three witnesses." If he refuses to listen to them, tell it to the church; and if he refuses to listen even to the church, treat him as you would a pagan or a tax collector.
>
> I tell you the truth, whatever you bind on earth will be bound in heaven, and whatever you loose on earth will be loosed in heaven.
>
> Again I tell you that if two of you on earth agree about anything you ask for, it will be done for you by My Father in heaven. For where two or three come together in My name, there am I with them (Matthew 18:15–20).

There are several important truths in this statement which are easily overlooked. Even traditional statements regarding church discipline from various confessions and statements of church order over the years, often miss things taught here.

There is no question that the first step in this process of reconciliation (for that is the primary subject in view here) obligates *every member* of the church. But just how far does this principle go? Does Matthew 18 apply only to cases of personal injury or offense, as some have sought to maintain?

I have heard pastors, elders, deacons and church members try to find every conceivable way to avoid dealing seriously with the subject of church discipline. But this text will never go away. The arguments I have heard used to explain this text often advance the notion that these words should not be *universally* applied. I would suggest otherwise for several reasons.

First, the larger context of this chapter points to a universal application. Earlier in this same chapter, in verse 7, our Lord said, "Woe to the world because of the things that cause people to sin! Such things must come, but woe to the man through whom they come." Sins will happen, Jesus declares, but woe to the one who causes them to happen. His solemn warning is followed by verses 15–17.

Then Titus 3:10 says, "Warn a divisive person once, and then warn him a second time. After that, have nothing to do with him." Is this an action to be taken *only* with regard to divisiveness in a particular situation? I suggest that it is far more likely that we have, once again, a universal principle such as that given in Matthew 18:15.

Furthermore, given all that the rest of Scripture says about discipline in the church, can we deduce a better way to deal fairly and honestly with the problems of human relationships within a congregation than that found here? The answer, to my mind, is obvious. The very spirit of Christianity itself demands a course of treatment not differing essentially from the prescription stated here.

In addition, several other passages in the New Testament add weight to the view that Matthew 18 must have both a general and universal application to the whole church family. Listen to James: "My brothers, if one of you should bring him back, remember this: Whoever turns a sinner from the error of his way will save him from death and cover over a multitude of sins" (5:19–20). And the words of the last chapter of Galatians add further evidence to my conclusion: "Brothers, if someone is caught in a sin, you who are spiritual should restore him gently. But watch yourself, or you also may be tempted" (6:1).

But Aren't We All Sinners?

But what truly constitutes a disciplinable offense in the church? None of us is ever entirely faultless; that is certain. Even though redeemed and declared just by God Himself, we remain sinners; i.e. *simul justus et peccator*.[8]

Precisely at this point we hear the familiar cry of "Judge not lest you be judged," or even "Let him who is without sin cast the first stone." Every time I have become engaged in church discipline, over the course of nearly thirty years of ministry, these words arise from some corner. So what does the serious church leader do?

I always begin by returning to a deep sense of my own poverty before the Lord. In doing so I am made acutely aware of His protective care, lest I fall into serious offense. I have learned, firsthand, that none of us can say, "I am above the possibility of ever facing such serious churchwide censure and discipline." Let the pastor, of all people, beware, for

---

8 This famous Latin phrase means, literally, "simultaneously just, yet still a sinner!" Even when Roman Catholic interlocutors granted much to Luther and the Reformers regarding grace and faith, this phrase expressed the important dividing line. Rome could not accept, and still cannot accept, the doctrine that says a person is right now perfectly just before a holy God and yet remains, at the same precise moment, a sinner in every way.

he too may fall!

And it must be continually remembered that not every offense demands formal church discipline.[9] The seasoned counsel of the past is again worthy of careful consideration:

> Even in those whose general deportment and conduct are such as to render their piety unquestionable, there may be found a thousand imperfections and weaknesses and blemishes of Christian character, so slight as not to demand a strict application of the rule. The correction of these minor and comparatively trifling evils is to be sought, not by those decisive disciplinary measures which, in cases of more flagrant misconduct, are indispensable, but by kind and brotherly suggestions, counsel and admonitions; and if these gentler methods prove unavailing, it would seem to be the part

---

[9] I have actually seen church constitutions and procedures which state that *every* sin committed by a member is ultimately deserving of church discipline. This aggressive response is clearly not called for by the whole of Scripture. Furthermore, experience proves time and again that this creates an environment that is anything but a family of forgiven believers who struggle together to grow in the fear of God. This scenario usually results in more independent churches who embark upon modern "reformation" by reacting against the previous non-use of the biblical teaching on discipline.

of charity patiently to endure what it has failed
to remove.[10]

When is Discipline Out of Bounds?

The apostle counsels us that "We who are
strong ought to bear with the failings of the weak
and not to please ourselves" (Romans 15:1). I have
personally seen church discipline that is out of
bounds. I even led my church, on one occasion, to
receive a person into our fellowship who, we believed, had been unjustly disciplined elsewhere. An
elder, a pastor, a strong influential person, can decide to go after someone, even with the goal of
"cleaning up the mess in his church." This is never
acceptable, even if the majority approves it.

People are told, for example, to "check in" with
a particular elder if they are having to miss church
services. Or a member with a "bad attitude" is
threatened with immediate excommunication if
she will not agree, with her whole heart, with the
pastor's teaching. Such examples abound, especially in an age of such extremes as our own.
These must be understood as abuses of true church
discipline. This cult-like abuse of authority will
more than likely abound in coming decades, as
culture morally collapses. But this awful response
is never a reason for not doing what is right.

---

10 Walker, *Church Discipline,* p. 111.

What Offenses Call for Discipline?

Students of this subject have generally agreed that there are at least five such offenses.

1. *Heresies.* In this light read and ponder 1 Timothy 6:3–5 as well as Titus 3:10–11.

But who, really, is a heretic?[11] Someone who does not agree with everything the church confesses and practices? I think not. We must be careful here not to confuse differences of interpretation with actual heresies. Throughout church history godly people have differed on various points of doctrinal emphasis, while still truly confessing Christ faithfully as their Lord. Heresy, we must understand, involves truths which are catholic (i.e., universal), truths which are essential to a right confession of the historical Jesus and of salvation by grace through faith. A heretic is one who ultimately departs from the historic Christian faith, either in doctrine or practice. A heretic can also be a divisive person who uses truth to push a case for something that creates schism.

2. *Whatever tends to disrupt the church's harmony*

---

11 It would seem that the only heresy that remains, in most churches, is the belief that there is such a thing as heresy at all. The word, in Greek, actually refers to the person who divides the church by stressing some opinion that separates brothers and sisters unnecessarily, and thereby creates followers of error.

(cf. Romans 16:17–18).

Anyone who seeks to set up his own party by fomenting discord and strife through a contentious spirit must be marked out according to Scripture. If such a person resists all appeals to desist from such activity, he must be disciplined by the church.[12]

3. *Open ungodliness that results in a direct refusal to comply with clear biblical duties.* I have in mind here the person who enters upon a course of moral and spiritual declension, and cannot be recovered through any of the usual channels of personal and private effort. As an example, consider covetousness.

But this isn't a sin we can so clearly see. Covetousness is a heart sin, isn't it? Yes and no. One who proves to be continually dishonest and follows a course of fraudulent behavior exhibits openly the results of previous heart sin. Would not

---

[12] More than one over zealous church has removed a person without actually following the biblical teaching on this matter. The person is put under some kind of "ban" without due process of biblical practice ever being used. It is announced, on a public occasion, that "the elders have dealt with a matter in regard to" a particular individual. The church is then told to understand that the person has left because of some problem, etc. This is *not* true church discipline but a coward's way of getting rid of those who simply do not agree with leadership.

a convicted extortionist, who has failed to openly repent, need some kind of public disciplinary response from the church of which he is a member?

And what about 1 Timothy 5:8? Here a man is delinquent in caring for his own family. He is described by the text as being *worse* than an unbeliever. If such a person will not repent, what is to be the church's response toward him? Becoming a "deadbeat dad" is not a minor problem. The church has a responsibility to correct such abuse.

4. *Personal offenses*. Matthew Henry, the marvelous commentator whose work has blessed a multitude over several centuries, wrote:

> If thy brother grieve, affront, contemn, or abuse thee; if he blemish thy good name, encroach on thy rights, or injure thee in thy estate; if he transgress the laws of justice, charity, or relative duties; these are trespasses against us, and often happen among Christ's disciples, and sometimes, for want of prudence, are of very mischievous consequence.[13]

It could not be more clear that such behavior is most clearly in view in Matthew 18.

5. *Gross immoralities*. Usually these are the first, and sometimes the only, sins a church responds to

---

13 Matthew Henry, cited in Walker, *Church Discipline,* p. 123.

with church discipline. Scripture views offenses against chastity as sins of serious consequence, both for the offender and the church. It might be well here to read again the words of 1 Corinthians 5, which were mentioned briefly above.[14]

Intemperance, profane lifestyles, and vices and crimes in general all fall under this category.

When to Restore?

One of the greatest joys in ministry comes when disciplined members are restored to the life and fellowship of the church. But both the timing and manner of restoration call for considerable wisdom. Let me explain.

On the one hand there is a contemporary tendency to rush to restoration upon simple profession of remorse. Though we must always be rooted in the grace and mercy of God in our response to a fallen brother, we must never cheapen grace by the failure to connect it with true repentance. Every situation is different; thus, leaders must seek God for present wisdom. As a rule the first expression of

---

[14] Cf. John H. Armstrong, *Can Fallen Pastors Be Restored?* (Chicago: Moody Press, 1995). I seek to show that pastors should be removed from their office in certain cases. Sadly, few agree in our time. Such was not always the case, as church history clearly shows. Reasons for removal are not limited to sexual sins alone.

repentance should be put to one simple test—time. If this expression of sorrow is real, it will last. We can be sure of this. If God is at work we can expect remorse to deepen, mature, and result in the peaceable fruit of lasting righteousness. Therefore, waiting is almost always advisable, for the benefit of both the church and the person.

The church, historically, has erred in two directions. The opposite problem of not waiting is to develop an attitude of unhealthy suspicion, an overly demanding spirit. Some people seem virtually unwilling to ever restore. They find it hard to believe a person is truly repentant. The early church faced this problem with those who recanted their faith under physical duress and then wished to repent and be restored after their failure. One can be sympathetic with this concern, to a point. This is especially true given the fact that many loved ones had paid the ultimate price for their faith, while this "repentant" person was alive and asking to be brought back into the visible church upon an expression of sorrow for his or her previous denial.

In modern situations in the West the issue is usually not the open denial of Christ. It is, however, terribly easy for people, in our therapeutic environment, to feel remorseful while at the same time remaining manipulative of people and events. It is always wise for leaders to be extremely careful in restoring too quickly. The church needs to be able to celebrate the restoration in the *same manner* in which it grieved over the exclusion. For this to happen the leadership must take both time and care with regard to its counsel. The body can be hurt by an improper restoration almost as easily as it can be hurt by the failure to discipline at all.

Generally, I believe the best time and place for the church to hear of actions taken regarding church discipline is in the context of the Lord's Table, or the Communion service. This, it should be remembered, is the family meal. In this same context it is generally best to deal with restoration. The family can be invited to rejoice and celebrate the restoration of a fallen family member. The sense of God's presence will generally be known by the gathered church if this counsel is followed.

Our First Concern

Once it has been determined that a "disciplinable offense" has been committed, then what? As we follow the steps of Matthew 18 we must be careful not to merely observe them in a mechanical way. I have seen such more times than I care to admit.

The first thing our Lord plainly instructs us to do is to go to the person in private. Unless the sin committed is already public, which will often be the case, your first concern must be to guard the good name and reputation of the person. Wise Matthew Henry counsels, "If thou wouldst convince him, do not expose him."

Begin your conversation by simply stating the facts as you understand them. Be careful not to judge motives! (This is difficult to do, but extremely crucial to the overall process.) You do not go to accuse, but rather to inquire, to ask questions. And all of this is to be done in a context of meekness and gentleness.

Keep your objective in constant view—you are seeking to "win your brother over." Those genuinely concerned for the person's well-being should respond as did the psalmist: "Let a righteous man strike me—it is a kindness; let him rebuke me—it is oil on my head. My head will not refuse it" (141:5).

But what if the person will not listen, and the facts still seem to indicate a serious failure? Should you return the very next day with several witnesses? Generally the answer, as I understand it, is no. If you are convinced that your words and pleas have fallen on deaf ears, the next step, it seems to me, is to withdraw and pray for a season. After this you might even go once again in private. This failing, take one or two other witnesses and speak with the offender again. Such witnesses should generally be church leaders, though there could be several clear exceptions. When this step is taken, an attempt should then be made to gain a clearer picture of the offender's view of things. Seek to treat him or her as fairly as possible and listen, listen, listen.

But what if the evidence still condemns the person and he refuses to hear the counsel of several? Then, and only then, should prayerful consideration be given to taking the matter to the whole church at an appropriate time and place. The church leadership *must* become involved if it has not previously been called upon to counsel the offending party.

Great care must be taken at the point of this last step. No charge should be rashly introduced as "new business" in a congregational setting. Any action taken must be preceded by great care and considerable prayer. Note also that the purpose in "telling it to the church" is to see if the person will listen to the whole congregation's collective counsel. Matthew 18:17 suggests, upon a more careful reading, that the charge is first brought to the church, then the church waits upon the offending party to repent, and only *after* the offending party refuses "to listen even to the church" (i.e., to heed the counsel to repent) does the congregation "treat him as you would a pagan or a tax collector." This last phrase, in short, means to treat the person as someone who is no longer a part of the church, i.e., as an unbeliever. This final step is what has been called "excommunication." This is because the person is now put out of the visible community.[15]

As far as practical matters are concerned, it has been my own experience that the offending party will most likely not attend the public meeting if the earlier steps have been properly followed. There would seem to be no specific reason for the offender not to be allowed at such a meeting as long as he is not allowed to hinder the process.

No matter what the circumstances, the church should seek unanimity of spirit and pray fervently. Personally, I have found that if the membership is taught properly and has been encouraged to love one another in a Scriptural manner, a meeting for the purposes of church discipline will generally re-

---

[15] In systems of church government which are presbyterian or episcopalian the process varies somewhat. It would seem to me, regardless of one's view of the church governmentally, that the congregation must somehow accept, approve, or be involved in the decision or the discipline will not have its intended goal, e.g., having the whole church treat the person as an outsider. However this goal is accomplished, the leaders must be careful in presenting and explaining the case before the whole congregation. There is no allowance in Matthew 18:17 for *private* matters of church discipline that the whole church cannot understand and support in some meaningful way.

sult in a deep sense of God's presence with the entire church. This is not surprising in light of Matthew 18:19–20.

No Time To Wait

But what if the offense is of such an aggravated character that it needs immediate attention? I have in mind here publicly known sexual sins or crimes brought before a court of law. In such instances a profession of repentance and brokenheartedness cannot be measured until some time passes. Only subsequent conduct demonstrates if the offender is genuinely repentant.

Augustus H. Strong properly notes that in the case of the incestuous man in 1 Corinthians 5:

> Paul gave . . . no opportunity to repent, confess, or avert sentence. The church can have no valid evidence of repentance immediately upon discovery and arraignment. At such time the natural conscience always reacts in remorse and self-accusation, but whether the sin is hated because of its inherent wickedness, or only because of its unfortunate consequences, cannot be known at once. Only fruits meet for repentance can prove repentance real. But such fruits take time. And the church has no time to wait. Its good repute in the community, and its influence over its own members, are at stake. These therefore demand the in-

stant exclusion of the wrong-doer. . . . In the case of gross public offenses, labor with the offender is to come, not before, but after, his excommunication.[16]

The Pastor

What if it is the pastor who sins? According to 1 Timothy 5:19 he is to be treated like any other member, except that even greater care must be used to establish the charges. There is no different standard for elders as to the procedure to be followed. The requirements for consistent character are higher in a pastor's case (cf. 1 Timothy 3), but when it comes to discipline the manner is essentially the same. Indeed, a church that allows its pastor to go undisciplined, especially in areas of morality, brings greater reproach upon its name in the community and invites God's discipline on its ministry.

Why do so many of our churches simply allow the erring pastor to resign and then begin a new ministry somewhere else, often within a few months? There was a time when denominations published the discipline of its pastors and gave notice of such to all churches. This action was taken to protect the flock, not to drive out the wayward

---

[16] Augustus H. Strong, *Systematic Theology: A Compendium* (Valley Forge, Pa.: Judson Press, 1907), pp. 924–25.

pastor. Today a pastor can fall in one place of ministry and quite easily move to another ministry, with few repercussions. A faithful church must not only discipline an unfaithful pastor, but must do all within its power to assist him personally and professionally in a proper manner.[17]

Treat Him like a Pagan

Once a church member has been excluded from the church, according to scriptural teaching we have observed, then how do we respond to him or her? Matthew 18:17 very clearly tells the church to "treat him as you would a pagan or a tax collector." What does this mean?

How are we to treat pagans? As those who are outside the church, i.e., outside of Christ and in need of the gospel working powerfully in their lives to produce both doctrinal and ethical change. Does this mean the excommunicated person is unregenerate? Perhaps, but not always. This is something which may not be revealed until the day of Christ.

I have personally seen excluded members repent and for the first time truly confess Christ savingly. I have seen several return to the church, believing they had fallen very far from Christ and

---

[17] Cf. again my book, *Can Fallen Pastors be Restored?* I cannot, of course, develop my whole argument here, but this matter is of grave concern in our generation.

openly desiring to be put right before God and man. Some have evidenced repentance for a short time, only to fall again. I have seen still others refuse all loving remonstrance and go headlong into willful sin and destruction. One thing is certain: I have never seen an excluded member, disciplined properly by the means outlined above, grow in grace, in the love of Christ, and in the fellowship of God's people.

It is most important that the *entire* church understand what exclusion really means. The church must be faithfully taught to understand that an excommunicated member has no relationship with Christ's church on earth and must be treated accordingly. This lack of association refers to having fellowship with that person as a member of the visible church, not an infallible declaration regarding the person's possible membership in the one true invisible church in heaven. The matter of the heart we must leave to God, but the matter of the sin must be judged and awaits true repentance and proper restoration.

It is at this point that the church will face perhaps its greatest hurdle. Long-term relationships and deep feelings for others often outweigh our obedience to the Word of God. Excluded members must feel their loss. For this to happen the church must act together as a united family. However, this does not mean we have to be cold or harsh in our response to excluded people. Years after exclusion I have personally continued to reach out, with expressions of love and interest, to unrepentant former members. I believe my response is called for by the Scripture.

When Discipline Leaves, Christ Goes Too

I confess that my belief in church discipline is strong. I do so because my confidence in the inspiration of the Bible is high and my commitment to holiness is immense. I will admit that church history gives sober reminders regarding the potential for abuse in discipline. Faithful followers of the Lamb have been excluded for their sheer obedience to the Word of God (e.g., the reign of terror by Bloody Mary, the use of excommunication against certain races or classes of people, etc.). But this is not my primary concern in this present generation. We have lived through decades of almost unimaginable permissiveness. This permissiveness now threatens to destroy the very witness of the visible church. As western society becomes more and more corrupt the question for us will be this: Will the church stand out from the world around it and be faithful to Christ as Lord?

John L. Dagg, a great Southern Baptist theologian of the last century, once commented that

"When discipline leaves a church, Christ goes with it." I believe Dagg was right.

Could it be that all the popularity and growth of the church in our day is a "success" that invites judgment? Our outward appearance is strong and rich while inwardly we are "wretched, pitiful, poor, blind and naked" (cf. Revelation 3:17). Should we not take care of what God has so clearly commanded us to do, and leave the matter of numerical growth to His own time and place? Have we compromised truth for what works?

In the book *New England Revivals*, Bennett Tyler recounts a number of firsthand reports of local awakenings that took place at the end of the eighteenth century in New England. One story has stuck with me, several decades after I first read it. Tyler recounts how a pastor led his church to discipline a very elderly man for living publicly in sin and in the defiance of Christ's will. This church, which had known coldness and dullness for years, finally experienced refreshing showers from on high at the precise time when it obeyed the Lord in church discipline.

One can only hope that a growing number of churches will again obey the Lord in this matter. Is it too much to ask that God would refresh us again if we will seek to do His will at all costs?

Recommended Reading

Adams, Jay E., *A Handbook of Church Discipline* (Grand Rapids, Mich.: Zondervan, 1986).

Armstrong, John H., (editor), *The Compromised Church* (Wheaton, Ill.: Crossway, 1998).

Armstrong, John H., *Can Fallen Pastors be Restored? The Church's Response to Sexual Misconduct* (Chicago, Ill.: Moody Press, 1995).

Clowney, Edmund P., *The Church* (Downers Grove, Ill.: InterVarsity Press, 1995).

Laney, J. Carl, *A Guide to Church Discipline* (Minneapolis: Bethany, 1985).

Owen, John, *The True Nature of a Gospel Church and Its Government*, vol. 16 of *The Works of John Owen* (London: Banner of Truth, rpt. 1965).

Walker, Warham, *Harmony in the Church: Church Discipline—An Exposition of the Scripture Doctrine of Church Order and Government*. Rochester, N.Y.: Backus Book Publishers, rpt. 1981).

White, John and Ken Blue, *Healing the Wounded: The Costly Love of Church Discipline* (Downers Grove, Ill.: InterVarsity Press, 1985).

Wray, Daniel E., *Biblical Church Discipline* (Edinburgh: Banner of Truth, 1978).

For her my tears shall fall;
For her my prayers ascend;
To her my cares and toils be giv'n,
Till toils and cares shall end.

Timothy Dwight

To Her My Toils
and Cares Be Giv'n

Donald S. Whitney on the Working Church

Working in the church is part of the pursuit of joy. Without this opportunity to serve Christ, joy is diminished.

During most of my engagement to Caffy (who is now my wife) I attended seminary six hours away. I wasn't around to take her home after work, to open doors for her, to run errands, or to do any such things that my love longed to do. My joy in her was incomplete because I wasn't able to serve her in so many of the ways I wanted.

Imagine being unable to serve your Lord through His church—could you be happy? What if the Lord told you that from now on you could attend church but not work in the church? If you are drowning in life and church responsibilities at the moment, the idea of someone releasing you from all service in the church might sound wonderful at first. But how would you feel a few weeks or months from now when you wanted to take part in some small way and were told you weren't needed? You volunteer to substitute-teach in a Bible study, but hear, "Thanks, but I have someone in mind."

The role you sometimes played in the worship service is now shared by several others, and the congregation seems to appreciate their ministry. You submit your name to serve in a number of capacities, but never get called. Those who enlist others to help in special events never contact you. You show up at various church functions, socials, outreach activities, etc., and while people are glad to see you and enjoy talking with you, no one ever asks or allows you to help with anything.

Could you bear to watch others' joy in the service of Christ while you did nothing? Wouldn't you nearly burst to "spend and be expended" (2 Corinthians 12:15) along with your Christian brothers and sisters? Wouldn't your heart ache to use your spiritual gift in some way with them for His glory? Wouldn't you long for some place of service, no matter how obscure, where you could express your love for Him?

And yet, during more than two decades of pastoral experience, the most relentless pressure I have faced, other than the continuous preparation for preaching and teaching, has been the constant need to recruit people to work in the ministries of the church. Just about everyone in the church says working in the church is a good thing. And everyone wants the church to offer a wide variety of ministries. But it seems as though only a small percentage of church members is willing to serve in ongoing ways so that those ministries can exist.

Is it a generational thing? While my experience is obviously limited, I have observed that the Christians of my parents' generation were strong on serving in the church, but weak in their private devotional life. "Saved to serve" was a slogan I often heard in church as a child. By contrast, my generation of believers strikes me as more interested in personal intimacy with God than in serving Him in His church. Did my parents' generation serve the Lord at the expense of knowing Him better? Has my generation overemphasized the individual and become self-absorbed?

Is it primarily a time thing? We're more rushed and overloaded than ever, obviously more so than a few years ago. Is the problem simply that people are barely treading water as it is, and don't have time to man an oar at the church? But if given the same amount of available time, would my generation devote as much of that time to the work of Christ as my parents' generation? Would a previous generation have given as much of itself to the Lord's work if it had as many attractive and competing choices as ours of how to spend its time?

The unending search for faithful church workers isn't just an American phenomenon. A well-known British pastor has written,

> It is a sad fact that there are many Bible-believing Christians who do not engage in any real work for the Lord. They loyally attend the services, and may give fairly generous financial support, but they *do* very little. They appear to be little more than comfortable observers. . . . Evangelicals generally have drifted a long way from the concept of every member being personally active in some avenue of service for the Lord. Indeed, some ministers have so despaired of getting back to the true standard that they now dismiss it as an impossible ideal.[1]

What is the true standard? Evangelicals maintain that the standard for Christian faith and practice is in God's inerrant Word. And within the pages of Scripture, perhaps the most concise statement of the Christian standard for serving in the church is in Ephesians 4:16. It begins by speaking of Christ, "from whom the whole body, being fitted and held together by what every joint supplies, according to the proper working of each individual part, causes the growth of the body for the building up of itself in love." God inspired the Apostle Paul to write here that every church member, that is, "every joint," is meant to supply some-

---

[1] Peter Masters, *Your Reasonable Service in the Lord's Work*, rev. ed. (London: Sword & Trowel, 1994), pp. 3–4.

thing to the rest of the church body. "Each individual part" of the church must be working properly for the church to grow and build itself up in love as God intended.

But verse 16 doesn't stand alone; rather, it is the culmination of a passage that begins in verse 7. The entire section relates to the work of a local church and the individual Christian's role in that work. It also reminds us that, as the Head of the church, Jesus Christ works in His church as well. Notice the emphasis here on what Christ has done, and what His purposes are:

> But to each one of us grace was given according to the measure of Christ's gift. Therefore it says, "WHEN HE ASCENDED ON HIGH, HE LED CAPTIVE A HOST OF CAPTIVES, AND HE GAVE GIFTS TO MEN." (Now this expression, "He ascended," what does it mean except that He also had descended into the lower parts of the earth? He who descended is Himself also He who ascended far above all the heavens, so that He might fill all things.) And He gave some as apostles, and some as prophets, and some as evangelists, and some as pastors and teachers, for the equipping of the saints for the work of service, to the building up of the body of Christ" (Ephesians 4:7–12).

Christ Teaches and Equips the Church through the Work of Gifted Men

The work of Christ in His church is described as giving gifted men to the church, namely apostles, prophets, evangelists, and pastor-teachers. His purpose for giving these gifted men is "for the equipping of the saints for the work of service, to the building up of the body of Christ." In other words, the Lord works in His church by gifting and calling certain men and giving them to the church so that through their work in the church the members of the church will do *their* work in the church (i.e., service) and build up the church.

The Apostle Paul later writes of "overseers" (pastor-teachers) in the church in 1 Timothy 3:1, "It is a trustworthy statement: if any man aspires to the office of overseer, it is a fine *work* he desires to do." This pastoral work of equipping the saints to do their work and building up the church as outlined in Ephesians 4:12 is further explained in the following three verses of Ephesians:

> until we all attain to the unity of the faith, and of the knowledge of the Son of God, to a mature man, to the measure of the stature which belongs to the fullness of Christ. As a result, we are no longer to be children, tossed here and there by waves and carried about by every wind of doctrine, by the trickery of men,

> by craftiness in deceitful scheming; but speak-
> ing the truth in love, we are to grow up in all
> aspects into Him who is the head, even Christ.

This means that those gifted by Christ for leadership in the church should *work toward the unity of
the church in both doctrine and experience with Christ*
("until we all attain to the unity of the faith, and of
the knowledge of the Son of God"). The "equipping
of the saints for the work of service" and the
"building up of the body of Christ" will remain the
work of ministers until a perfect unity becomes reality in heaven.

The unity here is not a uniting of faith and
knowledge, but unity experienced by the people of
God as their doctrine ("the faith") becomes more
pure and unanimous, and as their knowledge of
Christ becomes more intimate and universal. Most
churches tend to unify around either confessional
orthodoxy or shared experience and/or mission.
The former demand that all theological *i*'s be dot-
ted and *t*'s be crossed. Until that is in order, spiritual experience and closeness to Christ are rele-
gated to a secondary place. The other kind of
church rallies around one or more common spiritual experiences—whether conversion, charismatic,
or worship experiences—beyond which little adherence to particular doctrines is required. Sometimes leaders of these churches will plead, "Why

can't we just forget these doctrinal differences and get on with the Great Commission?" as though missions and evangelism can be accomplished without doctrinal content.

Unity grows as believers increase both in their understanding of the truth about Christ and in their experiencing of Christ Himself. So, on the one hand, the more closely their doctrine corresponds with the truth and with each other's beliefs, the closer they grow together. I pastored a church in the Chicagoland area for almost fifteen years. Though predominantly Anglo, our church was the most ethnically diverse of all the suburban churches in our denomination, yet we had wonderful unity largely because we had deep doctrinal homogeneity. Moreover, we shared much more in common with some of the inner-city churches in our fellowship than with some of the other suburban churches with our denominational label, because in both cases our doctrinal convictions superseded ethnic and socioeconomic comparisons.

On the other hand, no real unity exists between a true Christian and someone who isn't born again, regardless of the doctrinal context. Without the mutual experience of conversion, unity is impossible. As Paul put it in 2 Corinthians 6:15, "What has a believer in common with an unbeliever?" Moreover, even between two believers unity is more rich and sweet when both have a similar degree of "knowledge of the Son of God." For instance, two sisters in Christ who have experienced His nearness and comfort while suffering can share unity in the Spirit at a deeper level than they can with a new believer, as meaningful as that fellowship might be.

The balanced pursuit of unity found in experience with Christ and in doctrine is much like Jesus' assertion in John 4:24 when He said that those who worship the Father must worship in spirit *and* truth. The men Christ gifts to lead His church must work at building oneness through both spirituality *and* theology, heat *and* light, heart *and* head. The means for this work are the basics of pastoral responsibilities: teaching and preaching, as well as the ministries of discipling, counseling, and worship leadership.

Verses 13 to 15 also set before those who labor as leaders in Christ's church the responsibility to *work* toward maturing the members in Christlikeness. Follow the mandate from unity in faith and increased knowledge of Christ, to maturity in Christlikeness:

> until we all attain to the unity of the faith, and of the knowledge of the Son of God, to a mature man, to the measure of the stature which belongs to the fullness of Christ. As a result,

> we are no longer to be children, tossed here
> and there by waves and carried about by ev-
> ery wind of doctrine, by the trickery of men,
> by craftiness in deceitful scheming; but
> speaking the truth in love, we are to grow up
> in all aspects into Him who is the head, even
> Christ.

One purpose for which Jesus calls men to the ministry is to bring His bride to spiritual maturity. The measure of maturity here is "the measure of the stature which belongs to the fullness of Christ" (verse 13). Put another way, His will for us is that "we are to grow up in all aspects into Him who is the head, even Christ" (verse 15). Christ gives gifted men to the church for the purpose of making the church more like Himself. The church must become suitable to her Suitor. A holy Bridegroom requires a holy bride. This is the all-encompassing, never-finished work of the ministry.

Verse 14 says that, "as a result" of the unity and increasing maturity spoken of in verse 13, "we are no longer to be children." Jesus will not marry a childish bride, but a mature one. Part of the maturity He desires is doctrinal stability and discernment. Children are unstable and easily deceived, but "we are no longer to be children, tossed here and there by waves and carried about by every wind of doctrine, by the trickery of men, by craftiness in deceitful scheming." Of course, the way to build doctrinal stability and discernment is, once again, by preaching and teaching the Word of God. Of all that ministers must do in the church, this is their most critical and indispensable work. That's why "if any man aspires to the office of overseer" he "must be . . . able to teach" (1 Timothy 1–2) and is commanded to "preach the word" (2 Timothy 4:2).

This is the work Christ gives to those who are to equip the rest of those in the church for their "work of service." But Christ's plan is not a scheme of foremen and drones. The Apostle Paul saw the relationship of equippers to the equipped in this way: "Not that we lord it over your faith, but are workers with you for your joy" (2 Corinthians 1:24). Jesus gave ministers to the church for the *joy* of His people! The result of preaching the Bible and teaching doctrine should be *joy*. The unity of shared faith and experience produces *joy*. When equippers equip people for the work of serving God, the equipped should experience *joy*. When the people of God serve Him in the appropriate ways and with the right motives, the result is intense *joy*. That's why I began by saying that working in the church is part of the pursuit of joy and that, without this opportunity to serve Christ, joy is diminished.

But this is only one segment of a working

church. Let's turn from the work of the equippers to the work of the equipped. Once more, the beginning place is with Christ.

Christ Grows the Church in and through Loving Workers

Jesus Christ declared, "I will build My church" (Matthew 16:18). He has built it, and always will build it, both numerically and in holiness. Jesus not only builds up His body by giving gifted men who work in it, but He works in it through every member. As the Scripture puts it in the final verse of this section, Ephesians 4:16, it is Christ "from whom the whole body, being fitted and held together by what every joint supplies, according to the proper working of each individual part, causes the growth of the body for the building up of itself in love." Jesus is the ultimate church worker, growing His church by means of loving workers.

"According to the Proper Working of Each Individual Part"

Jesus does His work "according *to* the proper working of each individual part" of the church body. In other words, He works through and in accordance with the work of individual Christians to build up the whole. We do not grow the church; Jesus does. But He does so by working through all parts of the church body.

In verses 15 and 16 Christ is portrayed as the head of a body, and that body is His church. The individual members of His church are spoken of there as "joints" and "parts" of His body. So the Head—Jesus Christ—is the one who causes the growth of His spiritual body, but the parts of His body are not passive. The head on your shoulders causes the growth of your physical body, but it does so with the active involvement of your joints and other body parts. Your brain emits hormones and signals to the organs and nerves. Your head (via the mouth) sends food and water to nourish the cells and tissues. Your head is the cause of growth in your body, but the organs and cells must process the input from the head for the body to be strong and healthy. The joints must move to exercise the frame and the muscles for all the rest to be robust. In both the body of Christ and the body of flesh, heartflaps and kneecaps don't cause the growth of the body; the head does. If the body does not respond to the head, the individual members suffer. But when the parts of the body function according to the plan and directives of the head, there is health not only for each individual member, but for the body as a whole.

Let me turn your attention from analogy to application and ask: are you a working part of the body of Christ? Is your local expression of the body of Christ stronger and healthier because of you? You may have a high level of education or experience, or perhaps you know the Bible well, but are you vigorously using these blessings so that Christ can work through them to build up His body? The great British Baptist preacher of the 1800s, Charles Spurgeon, observed:

> As a rule we may measure a man's understanding by his useful activities . . . . Certain persons call themselves "cultured," and yet they cultivate nothing. . . . We know men who can distinguish and divide, debate and discuss, refine and refute, and all the while the hemlock is growing in the furrow, and the plough is rusting. Friend, if your knowledge, if your culture, if your education does not lead you practically to serve God in your day and generation, you have not learned what Solomon calls wisdom, and you are not like the Blessed One, who was incarnate wisdom, of whom we read that "He went about doing good." A lazy man is not like our Savior, who said, "My Father worketh hitherto, and I work."[2]

"Working"
    Jesus works in His church, and so do the

---

[2] C. H. Spurgeon, "The Sluggard's Farm," *Farm Sermons* (Albany, Ore.: The Ages Digital Library, 1996), p. 10.

healthy members of it. Thus we read in verse 16 of "the proper *working* of each individual part." Think with me about that word "working." Do you remember that verse 12 speaks of "the equipping of the saints" (and "saints" here refers to ordinary church members, not a special class of Christians)? The expressed purpose in verse 12 for equipping the saints was "for the *work* of service." Serving God is work.

I emphasize this because I have gotten the impression from some that, if you know your spiritual gift and minister in the power of the Holy Spirit in the place God intends, then service will flow effortlessly. But the truth is that even a person's "dream" ministry under the most ideal conditions (whatever they are) is done nevertheless in a sinful world and an earthly body, and so is still "the *work* of service."

If anyone knew the "right way" to serve God and build the church it was the head of the church, Jesus Himself. But even His service could be so physically tiring that afterward He could fall asleep in an open boat in the middle of a storm (see Matthew 8:24). The founder of so many churches, the Apostle Paul, wrote about the physical cost of his service for the body of Christ. In 2 Corinthians 11:23–28 he told of being imprisoned, beaten, lashed, stoned, shipwrecked, hungry, thirsty, cold, and deprived of sleep. He endured dangers from rivers, robbers, persecutors, and the sea. His description for all this was simply "labor" (verse 23), which is our English translation for a word that "emphasizes the weariness which follows on straining all of his powers to the utmost."[3]

Someone might think, "Well, that was for Jesus and Paul, not for the average Christian like myself." No, the words used to describe the labors of Jesus and Paul for the church are the same ones used for the service to God done by *all* members of Christ's church. So if Jesus and Paul found work for the church fatiguing, then so will you and I.

If you protest that for you to work in the church would take time from your pressure-cooker schedule and make you even more tired than you already are, I would give you two answers. First, I would say, "Yes, you are right." The "work of service" will sometimes make you tired. So it is with us all. Spurgeon was right when he said, "We cannot expect to serve the Lord, and yet have an easy time of it."[4]

Second, I would enthusiastically tell you that

---

3 Fritz Rienecker and Cleon Rogers, *Linguistic Key to the Greek New Testament* (Grand Rapids, Mich.: Zondervan, 1976), p. 491.

4 C. H. Spurgeon, *A Popular Exposition of the Gospel According to Matthew* (1893; Albany, Ore.: The Ages Digital Library, 1997), p. 21.

despite any exhaustion the "work of service" is worth it all. Surely you do not believe that Paul labored so exhaustively out of the shallow resources of sheer obligation! It was something greater than jaw-grinding duty that propelled Jesus to serve God's purpose and people at such cost to Himself. Both men were fueled by the fulfillment they found in serving an inexpressibly satisfying God.

One evening Jesus arrived about suppertime outside a city named Sychar. After walking all day, He sat down hungry, thirsty, and "wearied from His journey" (John 4:6). His disciples had gone into town to buy food, and a soul-thirsty woman passed them on the path in the opposite direction. She had come out to draw water from the well by which the weary Nazarene was sitting. As she brought up the water He asked for a drink. This began a conversation in which Jesus spoke the most profound words in the New Testament regarding worship and which resulted in the woman apparently believing in Him as Messiah (4:7–42). When the disciples returned and set a meal in front of Jesus, He said, "I have food to eat that you do not know about" (4:32). The spiritual pleasure Jesus derived from "the work of service" satisfied Him in a way that the tastiest food and a full stomach never could.

Food is necessary, but temporary. Rest and sleep

are necessary, but temporary. The satisfaction of having served God is eternal and without regret. The glory of the reward for it is as inconceivable as it is inevitable. How could any be content to merely attend a church and not serve in it when such joy and pleasure await them? How could any let the littleness and barrenness of busyness keep them from the transcendent satisfaction of a kind of work that lasts forever?

"The Proper Working"

Notice also that verse 16 does not advocate just any kind of work for Christ in His church, but "the proper (or, as some translate it, "the effective") working." As we've already seen, the proper motive is necessary for "proper working." A. W. Tozer argued, "In Christian service, motive is everything."[5] Poorly motivated, joyless service begets no glory, either for God or for His servant. How wonderful a Master can Jesus really be if we don't want to serve Him or if we serve with the glum face of a convict assigned to clean the prison toilets?

Proper working surely implies most often a consistent working. Neither a body nor a church works well when the members of it do not function consistently. Increasingly I hear church workers say,

---

5 A. W. Tozer, *The Next Chapter after the Last* (Camp Hill, Pa.: Christian Focus, 1987), p. 70.

"Call me if you get into a real crisis," or "I'll serve
in an emergency," or "I'll help when it's conve-
nient." But the church needs consistent workers,
not convenience workers. Today people are more
likely to lead a class, if at all, only on a monthly or
quarterly basis. What happened to the faithful servant who would teach a Sunday school or Bible
study class or be committed to some other ministry
for years? How much would your personal effec-
tiveness at your job or in your daily life be diminished if your hands or ears worked only one to
three months a year or only "in an emergency"? It is
no different for the church.

As I commented in the previous section, properly and effectively working in the church will also
involve costly—sometimes even radical—service.
The "work of service" often costs time, money, and
energy. Waiting until you have the time or other resources needed to serve in the church is like waiting until you can afford to have children. Such a
time never comes. Service that costs nothing accomplishes nothing.

"Each Individual Part"

According to verse 16, Christ grows the church
through "the proper working of *each individual
part*." The New King James Version translates this
as "each part does its share." The practical mean-

ing is that each individual part of the body of Christ, that is, each member of a local church, has a share of the ministry work to be done in that church.

It's not just that "each individual part" *should* work properly within the church, but each member *can*. That's because everyone who is a true part of Christ's body has been given a spiritual gift to enable and privilege him or her to perform effective ministry. When the Holy Spirit takes up residence in any human He brings a heavenly gift for earthly service. "As each one has received a special gift," reads 1 Peter 4:10, "employ it in serving one another as good stewards of the manifold grace of God." Thus every member—not just those in "formal" places of ministry, like pastor-teachers— has the ability and responsibility to minister in the church.

This balance is beautifully seen in a London church often remembered only for its preacher, C. H. Spurgeon. But the Metropolitan Tabernacle of the last half of the 1800s was anything but a mere preaching center. Through the gifts of their pastor-teacher, the individual members were equipped "for the work of service." Arnold Dallimore writes of Spurgeon's hearers that

> there were very few who came only on Sundays. . . . The Tabernacle was a place of al-

most constant activity. On each of the seven days of the week the doors were opened at 7:00 in the morning and did not close till 11:00 at night, and there were persons coming and going all of the time. . . . The Sunday school met in the afternoon. It was a fervent institution with well over a thousand boys and girls in attendance and something like a hundred teachers. . . . On Sunday evenings the number of Tabernacle people who were out conducting meetings amounted to at least a thousand. . . . As Spurgeon remarked, the Tabernacle was "like a hive of bees," and for the vast majority of its people to be a member meant to live a very busy life.[6]

With the gift given by God and the equipment furnished by Christ's equippers, "each individual part" of a local church should work properly in that church. Obviously we should manifest in all of life the Christlike character of a servant as part of our witness to the world. But the Lord's command through Peter to employ our gifts "in serving one another" clearly means to serve one another in the *church*. Serving in this way involves more than generally being servant-hearted to one another. To do that doesn't take a specific spiritual gift. Instead we should serve one another with our gifts, that is, *by*

---

[6] Arnold Dallimore, *Spurgeon* (Chicago: Moody Press, 1984), pp. 153–159.

means of our gifts. For instance, Romans 12:6–8 tells us that those who have the gift of teaching should serve by teaching, those who have the gift of mercy should serve by showing mercy with cheerfulness, and so forth. The specific opportunities to serve by means of our giftedness may differ from church to church, but the obligation and freedom to serve in some capacity remain.

In a message to his church on this subject, John MacArthur declared:

> All the spiritual gifts function in the *church*. The church is the place where spiritual gifts are supposed to be ministered. . . . It grieves me that people can be involved with a church superficially and have no ministry. They can be very busy in a whole lot of stuff that's going to burn—perish—and have absolutely no heart for what will alone last forever. Service—this [that is, the church] is the place for that, this is where that happens. When you become a part of a church you're saying, "I'm ready to serve."[7]

"The proper working of each individual part" is also described in Ephesians 4:16 by the expression "what every joint supplies." Church members are

---

[7] John F. MacArthur, Jr., from a taped message, "Commitment to the Church," GC 80–130. Grace Community Church, Sun Valley, Calif., September 1994.

like joints ("and ligaments," adds Colossians 2:19). And *every* joint supplies" something needful to the rest of the body. So if you are a church member and do not work in the church properly, the body lacks what you are meant to furnish.

I spent my seventeenth birthday in a Memphis hospital recovering from a football-related knee surgery. Before sending me home, the surgeon immobilized my left leg in a plaster cast. After only six weeks of my knee and ankle joints and their ligaments being unable to fulfill their role in my body, that leg had atrophied significantly. Just as every joint and ligament in every human body has a job to do *in that body*, so every member in the body of Christ has a role to fulfill in the local expression of *that* body. Otherwise that church won't be as strong as it could be. As the Lord did not make useless parts for your physical body, so also Christ has a ministry *to* the body *by* every part of His body.

When God makes body parts, whether for physical bodies or spiritual bodies, He makes them for a specific function in a specific body. Regardless of your educational level, IQ, experience, or talents, if you are a Christian you have a Christ-intended function in the church. You are there for a reason. You aren't there just for yourself and what you can get out of the church. God's plan for the church involves every member ministering to the rest of the church. For in this way each of us supplies something of Christ to the others.

"For the Building Up of Itself in Love"
Having come this far in our understanding of the working church, let's not lose the end among the means. So here's verse 16 again in its entirety, beginning with the last word of verse 15: "Christ, from whom the whole body, being fitted and held together by what every joint supplies, according to the proper working of each individual part, causes the growth of the body for the building up of itself in love." Christ works in His church through gifted leaders and working members to "cause the growth of the body for the building up of itself in love." Applied personally, each Christian could say, "Jesus Christ, working through people in the church, causes me to love Him and His people more."

Love is the ultimate virtue (1 Corinthians 13). Love for God and love for others are the two greatest commandments (Mark 12:28–31). When we speak truth in the church, verse 15 emphasizes, we're to be "speaking the truth in love." When the Apostle Paul spoke the truth of God's Word in the church, he did so to produce love: "But the goal of our instruction is love from a pure heart and a

good conscience and a sincere faith" (1 Timothy
1:5). Even though we have great spiritual gifts and
use them powerfully within the church, without
love we are nothing (1 Corinthians 13:1–2). We
may even perform great works of sacrificial service
or witness, but without love they profit nothing
(1 Corinthians 13:3). Jesus Christ wants a loving
bride. All that we do in the church, including the
exercise of our spiritual gifts and our "work of service," should be done to help make the church a
holy and loving bride for Him.

This is another way of stating what was expressed in verses 13–15. There the goal of the work
of ministers is maturity of the church members in
Christlikeness. As Jesus causes the church to build
itself up in love, He is causing the church to become more like Himself. So "the growth of the
body" Christ works toward is not simply adding
more people, but growth in the sense of more people becoming more Christlike, more loving.

True church growth is the result of the church
working as it should. When the leaders use their
gifts to mature the members in Christlikeness and
to equip them, and "each individual part" of the
body does its "work of service" properly, and all do
their work in love and to promote love, then all
forms of growth will occur. And Christ's ultimate
goal is to grow every member of His church more

into a reflection of Himself in purity and love. A pastor friend of mine in Illinois was asked, "Is your church growing?" I loved his response. He reflected for a moment and then answered, "Yes, I do believe we are more like Christ than we were at this time last year."

John Owen, the greatest theologian among the English Puritans of the sixteenth and seventeenth centuries, affirmed this as true church growth: "The great business of the church is not our number by addition, but by grace, by growing up in Christ. And the way whereby He doth it, is the working of every part, according to everyone's measure, for the edification of itself in love. . . . This we all know; but we are slow in the improvement of it."[8]

Improving the Working Church

So how can we, in Owen's words, "improve" our role in "the proper working of each individual part" and "the growth of the body for the building up of itself in love"? The most obvious starting point is to find a place in your local church and actually begin to do "the work of service." If none of the existing ministries seems to fit your mix of gifts, talents,

---

[8] John Owen, "The Mutual Care of Believers Over One Another," *The Works of John Owen*, vol. 16, *The Church* (London: Jonstone and Hunter, 1850–53; rpt., Edinburgh: Banner of Truth, 1965), pp. 477–478.

experience, and inclinations, perhaps the Lord means for you to begin a new type of ministry in that church. Then, having found a place of service, how can you "improve" on that?

Aspire to great work for God. In 1792 William Carey, the father of modern missions, preached a sermon based on Isaiah 45:2–3, coining the now-familiar aphorism: "Expect great things from God. Attempt great things for God." Why shouldn't you aspire to serve God greatly? Would you aim to serve Him little? How can anyone know such a ravishing, fulfilling, satisfying, and inexpressibly astonishing God and not long to serve Him wholeheartedly and sacrificially? Surely there will not be one regret at the Judgment for service rendered to God, except that we didn't serve Him more. Think of how willing Christians are to serve the companies that employ them, or their bosses (many of whom are unconverted). Should we serve Christ with less zeal? Should we save our best thoughts, highest dreams, and greatest work for them and not for the One who died for us and gave us eternal life? The Lord Jesus deserves our best love. He is worthy of our costliest sacrifices.

Aspire to great love for Christ and others as the fruit of your "work of service." As you do your work of service, think, "I want my service to result in people loving Christ more and loving others more." Don't just "do your duty" in serving. Don't just accomplish tasks. Have a greater, truer vision of your work. See your service as a means to an end. Realize that Christ has ordained your service as a means to the end of the church being built up in love. Consequently, if you teach, teach so that the goal of your instruction is love. If you set up tables and chairs, do it in a way that helps people in attendance to be taught to love God and others. If you work on a committee, help the group remember that the ultimate purpose of their work is to promote love for the Lord and love for the church. Whatever your "work of service," pray and labor for the luscious fruit of love to grow from it.

Aspire to great perseverance in your "work of service." Anything that is work, whether inside or outside the church, brings us sooner or later to the place where we think about quitting. The same is true for the "work of service." Criticism, fatigue, routine, hiddenness, lack of appreciation, stress overload—Satan will use all of these to tempt you to quit. Determine when times are good that, by the grace of God, you won't quit when times are hard. Resolve to serve Christ in His church as a consistent worker—not a mere convenience worker—as long as He gives you strength. And never think of retiring from the "work of service." The field or kind of work may change, but banish the thought of finding an easy chair in the church.

But perhaps nothing so erodes perseverance as the sense that your "work of service" is a waste of time. If you think your small or obscure work for Christ doesn't matter, His words for you are found in 1 Corinthians 15:58: "Therefore, my beloved brethren, be steadfast, immovable, always abounding in the work of the Lord, knowing that your toil is not in vain in the Lord." Rely fully on His assuring promise from Hebrews 6:10: "For God is not unjust so as to forget your work and the love which you have shown toward His name, in having ministered, and in still ministering to the saints." Work on! Again, to quote the great Spurgeon:

> Oh, when we get to heaven, if we could have regrets, would not this be one, that we had not served Him better? When we served the world, some of us, we used to do it very heartily. When some of you were in the devil's service, what bold soldiers you were! Nothing was too hot or too heavy in his cause. And shall we serve Christ with less zeal than men serve the great enemy of souls? Our Master deserves to have the best love, the warmest confidence, the sternest perseverance, the utmost self-denial—let us seek to give Him these, and to give them with a cheerful heart.[9]

---

[9] C. H. Spurgeon, "Serving the Lord with Gladness," *Metropolitan Tabernacle Pulpit*, vol. 13, (London: Passmore

Aspire to great joy through serving God. The call to service is a call to joy. When God converts a sinner, making him a new creation, He gives that person a nature that can experience delight in what the world would consider drudgery. Spurgeon explains:

> The vigorous healthy Christian must serve the Lord, ay, and serve Him with gladness too, because he is then obeying the instincts of his nature, and God has made our instincts, when we follow them, to be pleasurable. The instincts of the new nature, when we follow them out, lead us into service, and consequently there comes into our soul a pleasure unknown to those who are not partakers of the regenerate nature. I have said that to the Christian it is a delight to serve God, and so it is, because it exercises in him those powers which yield delight. . . . Believing service is not the performance of a work naturally irksome to us, to which we bring ourselves by effort; but Christian service is the doing of sacred duties, which to our new nature are congenial occupations, things in which we take our delights. The service of God is not to him an employment from which he would escape if he could. No; he feels it to be an intense delight, and only wishes that he could be more perfectly

and Alabaster, 1868; rpt., Albany, Ore.: The Ages Digital Library, 1997), pp. 623–624.

taken up with it.[10]

The Christian can find glory, splendor, and spiritual pleasure in the "work of service," for it is God's work. In the ordinary ministry of the church he can experience Christ working through him. Come, join us in this great work, the work of the church of Jesus Christ. Come, taste the joy as we "serve the Lord with gladness" (Psalm 100:2).

---

[10] C. H. Spurgeon, "Serving the Lord with Gladness," *Metropolitan Tabernacle Pulpit*, vol. 13, (London: Passmore and Alabaster, 1868; rpt., Albany, Ore.: The Ages Digital Library, 1997), pp. 616–617.

Elect from ev'ry nation,
Yet one o'er all the earth,
Her charter of salvation
One Lord, one faith, one birth;
One holy name she blesses,
Partakes one holy food,
And to one hope she presses,
With ev'ry grace endued.

Samuel J. Stone

One O'er All the Earth

R. C. Sproul on Church Unity

I like the hymn "The Church's One Foundation," but I do not like the first line of that hymn:

> The church's one foundation
> Is Jesus Christ her Lord.

Obviously, this plays on the building metaphor that is found in Scripture; but if you look carefully at that metaphor, the fundamental image that the New Testament uses, with respect to the foundation, is not Jesus. Rather, the prophets and the apostles are the foundation of the church. The foremost metaphor for Jesus is that He is the chief cornerstone, and there is no other foundation which can be laid except that which is laid in Christ Jesus—but He is the cornerstone. The prophets and the apostles serve as the foundation, and upon that is built the house of God. But note the rest of the first verse of that great hymn:

> With His own blood He bought her,
> And for her life He died.

Verse 2 of the hymn says that we are:

> Elect from every nation,
> Yet one o'er all the earth.
> Her charter of salvation
> *One* Lord, *one* faith, *one* birth.
> *One* holy name she blesses,
> Partakes *one* holy food,
> And to *one* hope she presses
> With ev'ry grace endued.

Verse 4:

> Yet she on earth hath union
> With God, the three in one,
> And mystic sweet communion
> With those whose rest is won.
> Oh, happy ones and holy,
> Lord, give us grace that we,
> Like them the meek and lowly,
> On high might dwell with Thee.

We can sing these hymns and really not pay attention to the words. And these are magnificent words, in spite of my statement above about the first line.

I once preached at a church that had two services on Sunday morning, an 8:00 a.m. service and a later one. The one at 8:00 was sparsely attended. When I came to that church to speak, there must have been about 20 to 30 people assembled in a room that was capable of holding 1,000. It was a little difficult geting energized for the service. I stood up and started by saying that any time I am called upon to preach in front of so many people, and have time to think about it, I become fearful and intimidated. The people all laughed, thinking that I was kidding. I told them that I was *not* kidding.

"Let's think for a moment," I said. "How many people are here this morning? Let's take attendance." People looked around. They could easily count 20..21..22..23..24..25, and I said, "Wait a minute. Let's go to Hebrews 12:18: 'For you have not come to the mountain that may be touched, that burned with fire and to blackness and darkness and tempest and the sound of the trumpet and voice of words so that those who heard it begged that the words should not be spoken to them any more.' "

Can you imagine a situation where the Word of God comes with such ominous power and force that the people plead with Him to stop His Word? Of course, the author of Hebrews is referring to that day in the history of Israel when God called the people to sanctify themselves, and to prepare for Moses' ascent on Mount Sinai. God declared the mountain off limits for the people and said that if any persons other than Moses drew nigh and touched the mountain they would die on the spot. Even if their animals touched the mountain they would die. The people waited in fear and trembling, and they heard the thunder, saw the smoke, and saw the lightning flashing as Moses ascended to that place to meet face to face with God.

But the author of Hebrews tells us that that is not where we are now. We are not in the wilderness any more. We are not in a place that is forbidden. He says, "You have come to Mount Zion, to the city of the living God, to the heavenly Jerusalem, to an innumerable company of angels, to the general assembly, to the church of the firstborn who are registered in heaven, to God, the Judge of all, to spirits of just men made perfect, to Jesus the Mediator of the New Covenant, to the blood of sprinkling that speaks better things than that of Abel." This is a passage we should keep in our minds every time we assemble for worship.

Any time the people of God gather on the Sabbath day for corporate worship, they are experiencing what the Apostles' Creed calls "the communion of saints." In that gathering is assembled not only those whose heads we can count visibly, but the assembly is joined by angels and archangels in the company of heaven. The assembly is joined by the spirits of just men made perfect, the spirits of those fathers and brothers and mothers and sisters who have been faithful in the past and who are now in the church triumphant, who have gone before us, who have spilled their blood in this world for the sake of the Christ. They are here in our assembly. Most significantly, we are visited by the Bridegroom as the bride assembles.

One of the most precious realities of the Christian faith is the unity that binds the hearts and souls of every Christian not only with Christ, but with each other.

At the seminary where I teach, students are required to learn Greek. Two of the first words they learn are simple, little prepositions. There is the word *en* and the word *eis*. Both of these words can be translated by the word "in," but, more specifically, *eis* means "into," and *en* means "in." How these words function with regard to the Christian's relationship to Jesus is as follows: When the apostles preached Christ, they would call people to believe not *in* the Lord Jesus Christ (though that is often how it is rendered in the English), but it is to believe *into* Christ. After a person has been reborn and comes to faith in Jesus Christ, and believes *into* Christ, then Paul speaks of that person's being *in* Christ Jesus—*en* not *eis*. So the transition is this: when you first believe you move "into" Christ, and after you move into Christ thereafter you are "in"

Christ and Christ is "in" you. That composes what we call the "mystical union" between Christ and the believer.

What is the charter of our salvation, according to the hymn writer? What is the fundamental basis for Christian unity as we find it in the New Testament? First of all, one Lord. Every time I hear sermons on Christian unity, and on the need for ecumenicity, the text cited is John 17, the high-priestly prayer of Jesus. I would like to look at a small portion of it, beginning with John 17:9 (NKJV): "I pray for them [His people]. I do not pray for the world, but I pray for those whom Thou hast given Me, for they are Yours, and all Mine are Yours and Yours are Mine, and I am glorified in them; and now I am no longer in the world but these are in the world and I come to You, holy Father; keep through Your name those whom You have given Me that they may be one as we are one. I have given them Your word and the world has hated them because they are not of the world, just as I am not of the world. I do not pray that You should take them out of the world, but that You should keep them from the Evil One. They are not of the world just as I am not of the world."

Note the next words: "Sanctify them by Your truth. Your word is truth, and as you sent Me into the world, I also send them into the world; and for their sakes I sanctify Myself." And He goes on to say, "that they may be one just as we are one."

What I hear in the culture today is that Jesus prays that we will be one, and that the only way we can be one is to forget about doctrine because doctrine invariably and inevitably divides. Our unity is in Christ and in Christ alone, and, once we have that, we have to steer away from doctrine because all doctrine does is disrupt loyalty and unity. Doctrine divides.

Have you ever heard that? Have you ever said it? I have, because it is true—doctrine *does* divide. But the culture today would like to say, "One Lord, many faiths, many baptisms." They want to interpret John 17 in this way: Jesus is praying that some day the Church for which He has died will experience unity; that there will be a oneness among His people that will overcome all these fractures and fragmentations and divisions that mar His body in this world; and so He prays for this future hope."

But Jesus does not just pray for the unity of the Church. He prays for the purity of the Church. He prays for the sanctification of His people. Is the means by which God sanctifies His people and purifies His Church studiously avoiding doctrine? No.

The purity of the Church, the sanctification of the believer, comes through the Word of God and the truth of God. Yes, truth divides: it divides the sheep from the goats; it divides the gospel from heresy; it divides the Christ from the antichrist. If we are not prepared to live in the tension of that division, we will have an extremely difficult time because this is the history of the Church. These are not minor things; rather, in every age and in every generation the Church has had to pay dearly to preserve the essential truths of the gospel of Jesus Christ. Ours may be the first generation in Christian history that is unwilling to do that, so immersed are we in the culture of relativism. Our culture says that it does not matter what you believe, as long as you are sincere. Our culture preaches the doctrine of justification by a contentless faith. That is not Christianity; that is not biblical faith.

Jesus' prayer in John 17 was answered. This hope for Christian unity for which He prayed is not some future, eschatological reality. It is present reality, because everyone who is in Christ, and in whom Christ is, is not only united with Christ, but is united with each other. There are Christians who are Lutherans; there are Christians who are Episcopalians; there are Christians who are Presbyterians; there are Christians who are Baptists, Methodists, and certainly in other denominations as well. All these truly saved individuals are in Christ. So in Christ these individuals are not only united to

Christ, but united to each other. There is a union among Christians that nothing in this world can possibly destroy, because it is a union that rests in Him, which union can never be broken.

The second part of the charter of salvation is "one faith." I wrote a book a few years ago called *Grace Unknown*. The purpose of that book was to try to give a summary of the essence of the Reformed faith. I was thinking of people who were in positions of leadership, such as elders in Presbyterian or other Reformed churches, and I wanted to give a summary of Reformed theology, to explain the five points of Calvinism, but also to point out that the five points of Calvinism are just one small part of the Reformed faith. There is a lot in Reformed theology that Reformed people share in common with all other Christians. Not all evangelicals are Reformed, but all Reformed people are evangelical. Not everyone who holds to "catholic" Christianity is Reformed, but everyone who is Reformed holds to that basic substratum of doctrine that is common to all Christians. We all believe in the Trinity; we all believe in the deity of Christ; we all believe in the atonement of Christ; we all believe in the resurrection of Christ; we all believe in the ascension of Christ. There is a common faith that keeps us bound together in the essentials of Christianity.

The distinctives of the Reformed faith are essential, I believe, for purity of doctrine, but not essential for salvation. You do not have to be Reformed in your theology to be saved, but I do not think you can be saved without being evangelical. That is why the term "evangelical Christian" is as redundant as the term "born-again Christian." How can you be a Christian if you are not born again? Jesus said that unless a man is born again he cannot even see the Kingdom of God, let alone enter it. Being reborn is a fundamental, necessary condition for being a Christian. So how can we distinguish between born-again Christians and some other kinds of Christians? Everyone who is a Christian is born again, and everyone who is born again is a Christian. And if your friends say they are Christians, but not reborn, what they are telling you is that they are not Christians.

It is the same with the term "evangelical Christian." The term "evangelical" means someone who affirms and believes and embraces the gospel. Think about it: can a person who does not believe in the gospel of Jesus Christ be a Christian? We can differ on all kinds of theological points, but, if someone rejects the gospel, can that person be a Christian? How can a person be a non-evangelical Christian?

We have a generation of "evangelicals" who do

not know their Bibles. I recently taught a course to 38 pastors who were from many different denominations. One of the requirements for entrance into this course was to have spent at least five years in ministry. I went to the blackboard and said, "Let's list the basic elements of the New Testament gospel so that, among ourselves, we can define and agree on what is the essence of the gospel." Two and a half hours later we did not have an adequate summary of the gospel of Jesus Christ. At that point someone finally thought to include the doctrine of the imputation of the righteousness and merits of Christ to the believer as an essential element of the New Testament gospel. He pointed out that we do not have the gospel until we have the way in which we receive the benefits of the righteousness of Christ.

A few years ago, a poll was taken on the floor of the Christian booksellers' convention of 100 people, who were asked to define the gospel. Only one answer out of 100 was adequate. Most people, when asked to define the gospel, will answer that Jesus died for their sins, or that the gospel means that I can have a personal relationship with Jesus. The devil has a personal relationship with Jesus; but it is a *negative* personal relationship!

There is content to the biblical gospel that has been lost and that has been eclipsed. I have objected to the original manifesto called "Evangelicals and Catholics Together," or, for short, ECT. It declares to the world a unity of faith and mission among evangelicals and Roman Catholics. What is declared is a unity in the gospel. I believe Romanists and evangelicals have many things in common, and they have common ground on which to stand on many issues; but the one thing that has divided evangelicals and Catholics for 450 years is the gospel.

That is what the issue was in the 16th century. It was not over some minor point of theological precision; it was the gospel. There is not unity on this, and, without the imputation of the righteousness of Jesus Christ, you do not have the biblical gospel.

I recently visited the city of Rome while leading a tour throughout Italy. I gave lectures on ancient Roman history, Roman mythology, and the way in which the Roman Empire has intersected historically with the emergence of the Christian community. The people who put the tour together asked me what I wanted the people to see in Rome. They said, "We have to see the Vatican, St. Peter's, the Sistine Chapel."

I replied, "I don't care about those things. If the people want to see those things, that's fine. The one thing I want to see, and that I want these people to

see, is the Lateran Church, where there are the sacred steps." Martin Luther, you see, had his existen-
tial crisis here in 1510 when he made his pilgrimage to the Holy City, hoping to receive a plenary
indulgence on behalf of his paternal grandfather.
When he arrived in Rome he was horrified by the
corruption that he saw. But, as a good pilgrim, he
went to the sacred stairs, which allegedly had been
the stairs to Pontius Pilate's praetorium, upon
which Jesus walked when He was judged. The
stains on them are allegedly Jesus' blood. These
stairs were not discovered until the 12th or 13th
century, and were supposedly brought back to
Jerusalem by the crusaders, who were somehow
able to identify the stains of blood in the 13th century as being Jesus' blood. They brought them back
and erected them in the Lateran Church, which is
the official see of the Bishop of Rome. I felt that I
had to go there because I wanted to walk those
stairs where Luther walked. I wanted to contem-
plate the overwhelming, crushing experience he
had when he cried out, "Who knows if it is so?"

I went to the Lateran, but I could not gain access to the stairs. The reason why I could not ascend them was that there was a throng of humanity—elderly people on their knees, with great pain
and difficulty—ascending the stairs one at a time,
kissing each one, saying the rosary as they went

along in this laborious effort in which it would take them 45 minutes or an hour to get from the bottom to the top of the stairs. This was done so that they could gain the promised indulgences that were printed on a sign by the stairs. The sign guaranteed indulgences to the pilgrims who made this ascent, and then went on to say that there was an additional staircase on the right-hand side, which is a replica of the original one; if the first set was too crowded a person could go up the second (though not real) staircase and get the same indulgence benefit.

I stood there and watched, and I wanted to cry. I thought to myself, "Where do you find people in the New Testament gaining the forgiveness of God by ascending stairs on their knees and reciting a ritual of the church?" How far removed this is from the gospel of Jesus Christ. The gospel is "good news," but the gospel of Rome is this: Upon your baptism you receive an infusion of grace *ex opera operato* that places you in a state of grace, which grace you must cooperate with and assent to in order to be justified. God will then justify you when you have cooperated with this grace so that righteousness is truly inherent in you.

In Roman Catholic theology, a person must be righteous for the grace of God to "count" him as righteous, as anything else would be "legal fiction."

That person is then in a state of salvation unless or until he commits a mortal sin. A mortal sin is called a mortal sin because it kills the grace of salvation which was given in baptism. If you commit a mortal sin, you lose your salvation. You do not get rebaptized; you go to the second plank of justification, and which Rome defines as the sacrament of penance, which is for those who have made shipwreck of their souls. You must make use of the church's power and the church's sacramental authority, so you go to confession and confess your sins and get priestly absolution. Then you must do works of satisfaction that at least make it congruous for God to restore you to salvation. You then have *meritum de congrua,* or congruous merit, which is a requirement to be rejustified. This will keep you in a state of salvation as long as you do not commit another mortal sin before you die. The recent Catholic Catechism says that if a person dies with any impurity in his life or soul, he does not go to hell unless he has committed a mortal sin. However, that person will go to Purgatory, the place of purging, where the fires of Purgatory will come down and cleanse him from impurities. A person may spend two weeks there, two months, two years, or 200,000 years there, until he gets out and goes to heaven. That is the "good news" according to Rome.

The Protestant "good news" is that God has sent His Son into the world as a perfect sacrifice for our sins, and His life of perfect, active obedience gains perfect merit for all who put their trust in Him, which righteousness cannot be augmented or diminished. What could you possibly add to the righteousness of Jesus? How much merit can you contribute to the merit of Jesus Christ? How full would the "treasury of merits" be if it rested simply on His merits rather than the merits of the saints? What more possible indulgence could you require than to have God declare you ·just in Jesus Christ, when He imputes or reckons or transfers the righteousness of Jesus to all who believe? The "good news" is that the righteousness by which you are saved is not your own. It is someone else's. It is Jesus', and there is no other gospel than that.

But today we have people from an evangelical tradition who are negotiating the "evangel" on every point. I believe the greatest theological crisis in our day is the crisis of the gospel. This could not have happened in any other historic moment since the 16th century. It can only happen when the people of God no longer understand what the gospel is. It can only happen when people say, "I do not want to get involved in disputes about doctrine. Doctrine divides." People have adopted a Rodney King theology that asks, "Why can't we all just get along?"

We cannot all get along when the gospel is at stake. That is why, when the Apostle Paul had to deal with this kind of crisis with the Judaizers in the first century, he was prepared to die for the sake of the gospel. He asked, "What do I do? Do I please men or do I please God?"

There is only one gospel. The Judaizers were preaching a different gospel, which is *not* a gospel. They were adding the works of the law to the gospel. They were basically saying that the righteousness of Christ is not enough to save you. The "good news" of the Pharisees and the "good news" of the Judaizers was not good news. It was bad news.

But if you look at Christianity as a religion of therapy for your psyche, or a religion of convenience, a religion of relationships with other people and fellowship, fine. If all you are concerned about is finding friends who will be kind to you and sensitive to you in your hour of need, or finding good counsel to cope in this world that is filled with trials and tribulations, then fine. But it really would not matter if it was Christianity or Zen Buddhism, New Age or EST, or anything else.

But if you are looking for salvation, if you are looking for reconciliation with God, what you need is the gospel. Because it is the gospel that is "the power of God unto salvation." It is not a preacher's technique. It is not how relevant the worship service is. It is not how exciting the methodology becomes.

In the history of the world, no one has been saved by the power of answering an altar call, or by the power of raising a hand, or by the power of saying "the sinner's prayer," or by the power of "inviting Jesus into your heart." That is not what saves you. It is the power of the gospel that God uses to redeem your soul. It is by faith that that power is wrought in you. Anybody can make a profession of faith.

If your confidence is in your raised hand or your response to a preacher's plea, or because you signed a card somewhere or said a prayer some time, you are on very thin ice. Justification is not by professing faith; it is by possessing faith. Jesus warned His people that you can profess it and not possess it. You can say the prayer and not mean it. You can walk the walk and not mean it. You can raise the hand and not mean it. But it is the gospel that is the power of God unto salvation, not three easy steps. What we need to start preaching to people is the gospel. Even your personal testimony is not the gospel. Your personal testimony may be a useful witness to which God might give a blessing, but it is not the gospel. The gospel has an objective content. It is about Jesus. It is what Jesus

did, who Jesus is and what Jesus gives us and how
we receive it. That is the gospel. If we are going to
have the unity of which the New Testament speaks,
it is one Lord and one faith. We have to be in
agreement with the essentials of the Christian faith,
at the heart of which is the gospel itself. That is
where the unity of the Church must be, and no
unity which compromises the gospel can be accepted.

Christ prayed that we would be one as He and
the Father are one. There is no compromise in the
Trinity, only perfect agreement based on accepted
truth. That is the unity for which we must strive.

Like a mighty army
Moves the church of God;
Brothers, we are treading
Where the saints have trod.
We are not divided,
All one body we:
One in hope and doctrine,
One in charity.

Fanny J. Crosby

We Are Not Divided

Phil Johnson on Denominations and Unity

"That they may all be one; even as Thou, Father,
art in Me, and I in Thee, that they also may
be in Us; that the world may believe that
Thou didst send Me." (John 17:21).

In a videotape titled "The Pope: The Holy
Father," Roman Catholic apologist Scott Hahn
claims the proliferation of Protestant denominations proves that the Reformers' principle of *sola
Scriptura* is a huge mistake. He says:

> Do you suppose that Jesus would say, "Well, once
> I give the Church this infallible Scripture, there
> really is no need any more for infallible interpreta-
> tions of Scripture. The Church can hold together just
> with the infallible Bible"?
> Oh, really? In just 500 years, there are literally
> thousands and thousands of denominations that are
> becoming ever more numerous continuously because
> they only go with the Bible. It points to the fact that
> we need an infallible interpretation of this infallible
> book, don't we?[1]

---

[1] A full transcript of the videotape is available on the
internet at http://www.ewtn.com/library/scriptur/POPE.TXT

A tract published by Catholic Answers makes a similar charge:

> The "Bible alone" theory simply does not work in practice. Historical experience disproves it. Each year we see additional splintering among "Bible-believing" religions. Today there are tens of thousands of competing denominations, each insisting its interpretation of the Bible is the correct one. The resulting divisions have caused untold confusion among millions of sincere but misled Christians. Just open up the Yellow Pages of your telephone book and see how many different denominations are listed, each claiming to go by the "Bible alone," but no two of them agreeing on exactly what the Bible means.[2]

This is a favorite argument of Roman Catholic apologists. They are convinced that the unity Christ prayed for in John 17:21 is an organizational solidarity that is incompatible with both denominationalism and independence. As far as the Roman Catholic Church is concerned, the only way true Christian unity will be finally achieved is when "separated brethren" (non-Catholic Christians) reunite with Rome under the authority of the Pope.

---

[2] "Pillar of Fire, Pillar of Truth," on-line at http://www. catholic.com/answers/other/pillar.html

Keith Fournier, Catholic author and executive director of the American Center for Law and Justice, sums up Roman Catholicism's typical view:

> Throughout Christian history, what was once intended to be an all-inclusive (catholic) body of disciples of the Lord Jesus Christ has been fractured over and over. These fractures threaten to sever us from our common historical and doctrinal roots. I do not believe that such divisions were ever part of the Lord's intention, no matter how sincere or important the issues that undergirded the breaking of unity.[3]

Fournier says he is "not advocating a false non-denominationalism or superficial irenicism that denies distinctives of doctrine or practice."[4] But note that he *is* suggesting that doctrinal differences, "no matter how important," should not cause organizational divisions. Moreover, fewer than 12 pages earlier, he had berated those who "fight over theology."[5] And just a few pages before that, he had expressed outrage at John MacArthur, R. C. Sproul, and Jim McCarthy for saying they believe Roman

---

[3] Keith A. Fournier, *A House United?* (Colorado Springs: NavPress, 1994), p. 37.
[4] *Ibid.*
[5] *Ibid.*, p. 25.

Catholicism's rejection of justification by faith alone is "doctrinal error."[6]

Notice carefully, then, what Fournier is saying: He claims he wants unity without "superficial irenicism," and yet he objects when anyone contends for sound doctrine or (worse still) labels Roman Catholic doctrine "error." It seems that the "unity" Fournier envisions is merely the same kind of unity the Roman Catholic Church has sought for hundreds of years: a unity where all who profess to be Christians yield implicit obedience to papal authority, and where even individual conscience is ultimately subject to the Roman Catholic Church.

Although Fournier politely declines to state who he believes is to blame for fracturing the organizational unity of Christianity,[7] it is quite clear that he would not be predisposed to blame a church whose spiritual authority he regards as infallible. And since the Roman Catholic Church herself officially regards Protestantism as *ipso facto* schismatic, Fournier's own position is not difficult to deduce. Although Fournier manages to sound sympathetic and amiable toward evangelicals, he clearly believes that as long as they remain outside the Church of Rome, they are guilty of sins that thwart

---

[6] *Ibid.*, pp. 21–22.
[7] *Ibid.*, p. 29.

the unity Christ prayed for.

Of course, every cult and every denomination that claims to be the "one true Church" ultimately takes a similar approach to "unity." Jehovah's Witnesses believe they represent the only legitimate church, and that all others who claim to be Christians are schismatics. They believe the unity of the visible church was shattered by the Nicene Council.

Meanwhile, the Eastern Orthodox Church claims the Church of Rome was being schismatic when Rome asserted papal supremacy. To this day, Orthodox Christians insist that Eastern Orthodoxy, not Roman Catholicism, is the Church Christ founded (and that would make Roman Catholicism schismatic in the same sense in which Rome accuses Protestants of being schismatic). One typical Orthodox website says, "The Orthodox Church is the Christian Church. The Orthodox Church is not a sect or a denomination. We are the family of Christian communities established by the apostles and disciples Jesus sent out to proclaim the Good News to the world, and by their successors through the ages."[8]

All these groups regard the church primarily as a visible, earthly organization. Therefore they can-

---

[8] http://www.orthodox.co.uk/EOC.htm

not conceive of a true spiritual unity that might exist across denominational lines. They regard all other denominations as schismatic rifts in the church's organizational unity. And if *organizational* unity was what Christ was praying for, then the very existence of denominations would indeed be a sin and a shame. That's why the Orthodox website insists, "The Orthodox Church is not a sect or a denomination."

Furthermore, if their understanding of the principle of unity is correct, then whichever organization can legitimately claim to be the church founded by Christ and the apostles is the "one true Church," and all others are guilty of schism, regardless of any other doctrinal or biblical considerations.

That is precisely why many Catholics and Eastern Orthodox have focused their rhetoric on "unity." Both sincerely believe that, if they can establish the claim that they, and no one else, are the one true Church instituted by Christ, then all other Protestant claims about doctrine, church polity, and ecclesiastical abuses become moot. If they can successfully sell their notion that the "unity" of John 17:21 is primarily an *organizational* unity, they should in effect be able to convince members of denominational and independent churches to reunite with the Mother Church regardless of whether she is right or wrong on other matters.

The plea for unity may at first may sound magnanimous and charitable to Protestant ears (especially coming from a church with a long history of enforcing her will by Inquisitions). But when the overture is being made by someone who claims to represent the One True Church, the call for "unity" turns out to be nothing but a kinder, gentler way of demanding submission to the Mother Church's doctrine and ecclesiastical authority.

Nonetheless, in recent years many gullible Protestants have been drawn into either Catholicism or Eastern Orthodoxy by the claim that one or the other represents the only Church Christ founded. Having bought the notion that the unity Christ prayed for starts with organizational unity, these unsuspecting proselytes naturally conclude that whichever church has the most convincing pedigree must be the only church capable of achieving the unity Christ sought—and so they join up. Many recent converts from evangelicalism will testify that the proliferation and fragmentation of so many Protestant denominations is what first convinced them that Protestant principles must be wrong.

The Danger of Schism

This is not an issue Protestants can easily sweep

aside. It is quite true that schism is sinful. The Apostle Paul rebuked the Corinthians for having a sectarian spirit: "Each one of you is saying, 'I am of Paul,' and 'I of Apollos,' and 'I of Cephas,' and 'I of Christ.' Has Christ been divided? Paul was not crucified for you, was he? Or were you baptized in the name of Paul?" (1 Corinthians 1:12–13). Later in the epistle he added, "For when one says, 'I am of Paul,' and another, 'I am of Apollos,' are you not mere men? What then is Apollos? And what is Paul? Servants through whom you believed, even as the Lord gave opportunity to each one" (3:4-5).

Schism is a demonic sin, so much so that divisive people are not to be tolerated in the church. In Matthew 18, Christ outlined a series of four steps churches should go through in calling a sinning brother to repentance. But when someone is schismatic, Paul says, that disciplinary process may be accelerated. He wrote in Titus 3:10–11: "Reject a factious man after a first and second warning, knowing that such a man is perverted and is sinning, being self-condemned."

It's fair to ask, then, if schism is such a serious sin, why are there so many different denominations? The Protestant Reformation gave rise to Lutheranism, Presbyterianism, Anglicanism, Congregationalism, Methodism, Episcopalianism, the Plymouth Brethren, the Open Brethren, the Closed

Brethren, the Church of Christ, the Church of the
Nazarene, the Church of God, the Assemblies of
God, Holiness churches, Pentecostal churches,
Dutch Reformed churches, Christian Reformed
churches, Protestant Reformed churches, Baptists,
Reformed Baptists, Sovereign Grace Baptists, Land-
mark Baptists, Independent Baptists, American
Baptists, Southern Baptists, Freewill Baptists,
General Baptists, Regular Baptists, Particular
Baptists, and Strict and Particular Baptists.

And that list only scratches the surface. The
Handbook of Denominations lists hundreds more.
The sign in front of one Arkansas church adver-
tises: "The Strict and Particular Reforming Baptist
(Non-instrumental, Closed Communion) King
James Only Community Church." Are so many dif-
ferent denominational tags really necessary?

Let's be honest: one can hardly blame non-
Christians for being nonplussed by the variety. The
pagan from a non-Christian society is not likely to
look at Christendom and say, "Behold, how they
love one another."

The Necessity of Separation

On the other hand, we who are Christians must
understand that Christendom is not "the Church."
All who call themselves Christians are not true followers of Christ, and there's no reason that we

should try to make Moslems or Hindus think that all varieties of so-called Christianity are truly Christian. Just because a church or denomination calls itself "Christian" does not mean it is part of the body of Christ. That has been true even from biblical times. Consider, for example, the seven churches in Revelation 2 and 3. At least one was totally apostate, and three or four others were already apostatizing. We know from Jesus' warning to the church at Laodicea that it is possible for a church to abandon the truth so completely that Christ Himself will reject that church and spew it out of His mouth. True Christians must not fellowship with such apostate groups (2 Corinthians 6:15–17; Ephesians 5:11).

In other words, some degree of doctrinal purity is a valid prerequisite for organizational unity. It's simply wrong to set aside all our doctrinal differences for the sake of an artificial organizational "unity." This is particularly true of those doctrinal issues that are immediately germane to the gospel. In fact, the Apostle Paul taught that so-called "Christians" who corrupt or compromise the utter freeness of justification are not to be regarded as brethren at all! He pronounced a curse on them (Galatians 1:8–9). The Apostle John taught the same thing (2 John 7–11).

Since the major point at issue between Protestants and Catholic or Orthodox traditions is the gospel—particularly the doctrine of justification by faith, which is the very point Paul wrote to defend in his epistle to the Galatians—it is utterly fatuous to suggest that a show of external unity should take precedence over our doctrinal differences. It is tantamount to saying that Christians are not supposed to be concerned with truth at all.

The Wrong Kind of "Unity"

But the unity Christ prayed for in the Church is not, to begin with, an organizational unity. When Jesus prayed that we all might be one, He was describing a spiritual unity. In John 17:11, He prayed "that they may be one, even as We are." Verse 21 continues: "that they may all be one; *even as Thou, Father, art in Me, and I in Thee, that they also may be in Us*" (emphasis added). That describes a very specific kind of spiritual unity that proceeds from our union with Christ. Christ Himself likens it to the unity between Father and Son. It is certainly not something as mundane and superficial as the homogenization of all churches under one earthly hierarchy of bishops in Rome or Constantinople.

Organizational unity cannot guarantee true spiritual unity, and the proof is seen in the Church of Rome herself. Despite all the Catholic finger-wagging about the lack of unity reflected in

Protestant denominationalism, there may well be more disharmony within the Roman Catholic Church than there is on the outside.

Take, for example, Catholic Answers, the apologetics organization headed by Karl Keating. Although Keating and Catholic Answers did not invent the argument that Protestant denominationalism disproves *sola fide,* they certainly have perfected and popularized it. Staff apologists from Catholic Answers are the chief ones who brought this issue to the forefront of the Catholic-Protestant debate. Catholic Answers published the tract cited at the beginning of this chapter. And Keating himself personally trained a number of pro-Catholic debaters to employ this argument in their dialogues with Protestants. Catholic Answers has hammered this same theme for years. According to them, an infallible, magisterial interpretation of Scripture is the only thing that can assure true unity, and the continuing proliferation and fragmentation of Protestant denominations is living proof that there can be no unity under the principle of sola fide.

Suppose for the sake of argument we grant their premises and measure Catholic Answers by their own standard? Keating and his stable of apologists say they have an infallible interpretation of Scripture, given to them through the magisterium of

Rome. So how has the principle of unity fared in their little group?

Not very well, it turns out. To give one well-known example, Keating has disavowed and waged war on the Internet against one of his best-known former lieutenants, Gerry Matatics, who now heads an organization of his own. (Several of Keatings former employees have left Catholic Answers and joined or founded competing organizations.). Matatics, it seems, prefers traditional Catholicism with a Latin Mass, while Keating is in favor of the innovations instituted by the Vatican II Council, including the new Mass in the vernacular. Keating now says he considers Matatics a "sad example of how how schism leads to heresy."[9] Keating has published articles in *This Rock* magazine warning other Catholics against his former associate's influence.[10] Meanwhile, Matatics insists that he remains loyal to the Catholic Church. And, in fact, not only has he remained in communion with Rome, but he has also enlisted several other influential Catholic leaders who have come to his defense against Keating's charges. Both sides have taken their case to the World Wide

---

[9] *The Wanderer,* February 16, 1995, p. 7.
[10] Karl Keating, "Habemus Papum?" *This Rock* (July/August 1995).

Web, posting articles and open letters, debating whether Keating or Matatics best represents the "Catholic" position.[11] The quarrel is more than four years old as of this writing.

The Keating-Matatics feud is symptomatic of several larger conflicts within the Catholic church. Keating is a "conservative Catholic," whereas Matatics is a "traditionalist." The traditionalists held sway until Vatican II, but since then conservative and moderate voices within the church have insisted that they represent "true" Catholicism. Traditionalists have formed their own sects within the church, such as The Priestly Society of St. Pius X, a traditionalist organization that opposes innovations in Catholic worship. There are also several Marian sects, including devotees of the various apparitions at Bayside and Fatima. Many of them disagree vehemently with other Catholics about the direction in which the Catholic church should go. Numerous other factions and sects operate within the walls of the Catholic church, waging polemic battles as lively and intense as any that ever took place between Protestant denominations.

Add into that mix the scores of modernist and liberal priests who would like to introduce their

---

11 See, for example, "An Open Letter to Mr. Gerry Wells in Defense of Gerry Matatics" at: http://members.aol.com/ MORRISTH/essays/gerry1.html

peculiar preferences into the Catholic system, and
you have a chaos of varying opinions that is at
least equal to that of the Protestants. The simple
fact is that there is really no more unity of agreement among Roman Catholics than there is among
Protestants. Even with an "infallible interpretation"
of Scripture, it seems, the Roman Catholic track
record on unity is as bad as, or worse than, that of
the Protestants.

How much "unity" can there be, for example, between Father Andrew Greeley and Mother Angelica
(to name two of America's best-known Catholics)?
Greeley is a liberal priest and novelist, who once
said on "Larry King Live" that he believes the
Catholic church eventually will not only ordain
women as priests, but also elect a woman as pope.
Mother Angelica is a traditionalist Franciscan nun
who has used her televised talk show to criticize
other Catholic leaders, including Cardinal Richard
Mahoney, for their non-traditionalist stance on
liturgical matters. Do Catholic critics of Protestant
denominationalism imagine that their church really embodies the kind of unity for which Christ
prayed?

In fact, with so many who profess loyalty to
Peter's chair waging battle among themselves over
key points of truth, it should be painfully obvious
to all that Roman Catholics are really no more able

to interpret their church's "infallible interpretation" than they believe Protestants can interpret Scripture itself.

And clearly, an external, organizational unity cannot guarantee the kind of spiritual unity Christ was praying for. It would be a serious mistake—and a serious blow to real unity—to imagine that the answer to our denominational division is the abandonment of denominations altogether, and the union of all who profess Christ into one massive worldwide organization where we affirm only what we all agree on. No real agreement whatsoever would be achieved through such means. Meanwhile, the cause of truth would suffer a severe blow, and that would ultimately prove fatal to all genuine unity.

The unity Scripture calls us to is a unity in *truth*. Paul wrote, "Now I plead with you, brethren, by the name of our Lord Jesus Christ, that you all speak the same thing, and that there be no divisions among you, but that you be perfectly joined together in the same mind and in the same judgment" (1 Corinthians 1:10). He did not counsel the Corinthians to grasp for a superficial unity by setting truth aside and embracing an organizational unity without regard to sound doctrine. Nor did Paul order them to abandon their differences and simply place a blind and implicit trust in his apostolic magisterium. He was urging them to work through their differences and strive to achieve unity in both heart and mind. Such unity is possible only when people are themselves in union with Christ. "For who has known the mind of the Lord, that he will instruct Him? But we have the mind of Christ" (1 Corinthians 2:16).

That is precisely the kind of unity Christ was praying for. There is nothing superficial about it. It is a unity of spirit. It is a unity in truth. And that is why, in the context of His prayer for unity, Christ also prayed, "Sanctify them in the truth; Your word is truth" (John 17:17).

Unity across Denominational Lines

Here's a fact many miss: To a very large degree, the unity Christ prayed for does exist among genuine believers, and it is a unity that transcends denominational lines. All Christians are "in Christ"; therefore they are all one with the Father, and one with each other as well. Notice carefully what Christ says in verses 22–23: "[I pray] that they may be one, just as We are one; I in them and You in Me, that they may be perfected in unity." The basis of that unity is not a denominational affiliation; it is our position in Christ.

Faithful evangelical Protestants believe God is answering that prayer of Christ even now. We enjoy an amazing degree of unity with one another, despite our denominational distinctions. In other words, the kind of spiritual unity Christ prayed for *does* exist in the true body of Christ worldwide despite denominational barriers. Our Lord's prayer for His Church has not gone unanswered.

Christ's true Church is not confined to a single congregation, denomination, or earthly organization. The Church is composed of all true believers in Christ, regardless of denominational affiliation or membership in any earthly assembly. In the words of the Westminster Confession of Faith, "The catholic or universal church, which is invisible, consists of the whole number of the elect, that have been, are, or shall be gathered into one, under Christ the Head thereof; and is the spouse, the body, the fullness of Him that filleth all in all" (25.1). When the Confession speaks of the Church as "invisible," it does not mean the Church is inconspicuous or utterly hidden from view. It means that its precise boundaries cannot be detected through human perception. There are people who claim to be, and appear to be, part of the body, but they are not. Others, perhaps unknown to us, are true believers and members of the body. The exact boundaries of the true Church are not always easy to discern. But nonetheless genuine believers are "all one in Christ Jesus" (Galatians 3:28), united with Him and therefore united with one another. "For even as the body is one and yet has many members, and all the members of the body, though they are many, are one body, so also is Christ. For by one Spirit we were all baptized into one body" (1 Corinthians 12:12–13).

During His earthly ministry, Christ told the disciples: "I have other sheep, which are not of this fold; I must bring them also, and they will hear My voice; and they will become one flock with one shepherd" (John 10:16). The "one shepherd" is Christ Himself, not an earthly vicar. And the "one flock" is a spiritual reality even now, with believing Jews and Gentiles united in one new body, and the middle wall of partition between Jew and Gentile having been broken down (Ephesians 2:14–16). The perfect manifestation of that unity awaits fulfillment in a future time, when "we all attain to the unity of the faith, and of the knowledge of the Son of God, to a mature man, to the measure of the stature which belongs to the fullness of Christ" (Ephesians 4:13). In the meantime, to settle for the superficial unity imposed by a monstrous worldwide ecclesiastical hierarchy would be a serious mistake.

The unity Christ prayed for has always existed in the true body of Christ. It is an organic, not an organizational unity. It is a spiritual, not a corporeal unity. And it is not a unity without diversity. (If He had wanted unity with no diversity, He would not have gifted us with different spiritual gifts.) But the kind of unity Christ prays for is a unity in spite of our great diversity.

The truth is that on the vital issues there is far more agreement among Protestants than Catholic and Eastern Orthodox church leaders would like to admit. All evangelical Protestants are in agreement on the doctrine of justification by faith (*sola fide*) and the authority of Scripture (*sola Scriptura*). (For helpful further reading, see the Soli Deo Gloria publications on those two key issues, *Justification by Faith ALONE* and *Sola Scriptura*.)

Proof that unity is the rule among believers despite their denominational differences can be seen in a survey of the denominational backgrounds of the men who have contributed to this book. There are Baptists of different persuasions, Presbyterians of different denominations, Dutch Reformed, and Christian Reformed. We may not always agree on every point and every particular of secondary doctrinal questions, but on the essential gospel truths we are in full agreement. And our unity in Christ is unbroken by denominational lines between us. We embrace one another with sincere love as members of the one body of Christ. We are one in Christ.

The school where I studied is an interdenominational school. My professors were Presbyterians, Baptists, Congregationalists, and Independents. Students came from an incredibly diverse array of Protestant denominations. We prayed together, studied together, and did evangelistic work together. Our denominational differences were no barrier to our unity in Christ.

The church of which I am now a member is a nondenominational church. Our members come from backgrounds as varied as Baptist, Brethren, and Presbyterian congregations. Our pastor is regularly asked to speak in all kinds of denominational settings. In recent years he has spoken in Anglican churches, Baptist conventions, Presbyterian conferences, and even Charismatic congregations. We do enjoy a tremendous unity with all those who truly love Christ and are faithful to His Word, regardless of our denominational differences.

The limits on this transdenominational unity are set by Scripture itself. We cannot welcome into our circle of fellowship people who deny truths that are essential to the gospel (2 John 7–11); and we cannot embrace people who affirm a gospel Scripture condemns (Galatians 1:18–19). The gospel and all truths essential to it are therefore nonnegotiable points of doctrine, and unity on these matters is a prerequisite to any other kind of unity.

But there's nothing inherently sinful with holding denominational convictions on secondary issues. Denominations in and of themselves are not necessarily an obstacle to true Christian unity, and Protestants should not be bullied into conceding otherwise. Of course, when denominational convictions on secondary issues are employed to promote strife and hostility between brothers and sisters in Christ, that is sectarianism. It's the very attitude Paul condemned in Corinth when some of the believers there were dividing in groups loyal to Paul, or Apollos, or Cephas, and refusing fellowship to members of the competing groups. Such sectarianism is certainly sinfully divisive. But it is not a necessary result of denominationalism. And those of us with broad denominational associations and close friendships in Christ across denominational boundaries are living proof of that.

There is room for brethren to disagree within the bonds of unity, and sometimes those disagreements can be sharp (cf. Acts 15:36–39). In fact, it is unlikely that there are any two Christians anywhere who will agree completely on the meaning of every passage of Scripture. Unity does not mean that we must agree up front on every point of truth. But unity certainly does not mean that we should ignore the issue of truth altogether and settle for a superficial organizational unity.

Great things He hath taught us,
Great things He hath done,
And great our rejoicing
Thru Jesus the Son;
But purer and higher
And greater will be
Our wonder, our transport
When Jesus we see.

Fanny Crosby

Great Things He Hath Taught Us

Joseph E. Pipa on the Importance of Creeds and Confessions in the Church

Introduction

Some of the most tragic words in the Bible are those that describe the condition of the church in the days of the judges: "Everyone did what was right in his own eyes" (Judges 21:25). These words described an absolutely devastating spiritual anarchy. Our days are marked by the same anarchy, not only in the culture, but also in the church. Congregations and individuals are doing their own thing. One congregation excommunicates a man for immorality. He goes down the street to another congregation that not only receives him, but even makes him an officer. Or increasingly, as "Christians" get unbiblical divorces, part of the divorce agreement determines which party stays in the local church and which one must attend another congregation.

A significant contributing factor to this anarchy and a consequence of it as well is the commonly heard protestation, "No creed but the Bible, no confession but Jesus." A great majority of Christians, as well as congregations, reject out of hand creeds and confessions. They do so because they believe that the Bible alone is sufficient to guide us and that creeds are man-made additions to the Bible. In this chapter, I will seek to demonstrate that the Bible commands the church to make and use creeds; to explain something of their purpose; and to show how we are to make our confession. My remarks are based on 2 Timothy 1:13–14.

First, though, I will give a definition, so that we may agree on what we are discussing. We derive the term "creed" from the Latin word *credo,* which means, "I believe." Your personal "creed" states what you believe and what is important to you. Thus, in reality, the statement, "No creed but the Bible" is a personal creed. You are saying, "I *believe* that neither I nor the church needs a creed. The Bible alone is sufficient to guide me." As I shall demonstrate below, no conflict exists between the doctrine of the sufficiency of Scripture and the use of creeds.

Throughout history, the Church has used creeds to summarize what she believed the Bible taught. Her creeds and confessions gave a precise summary of cardinal doctrines (the Apostles' Creed) or a detailed refutation of error and articulation of a particular truth under attack (the Nicene Creed). R. L. Dabney defines a creed:

> [I]t is a summary statement of what some reli-
> gious teacher or teachers believe concerning
> the Christian system, stated in their own
> uninspired words. But they claim that these
> words fairly and briefly express the true sense
> of the inspired words. The church records
> several creeds of individual Christian teachers;
> but the creeds of the modern Protestant world
> are documents carefully constructed by some
> church courts of supreme authority in their
> several denominations, or by some learned
> committee appointed by them and then for-
> mally adopted by them as their doctrinal stan-
> dard.[1]

Examples of creeds and confessions are the
Apostles' Creed, the Nicene Creed, the Heidelberg
Catechism, the Westminster Confession of Faith,
the London Confession of 1689 (a Baptist confession), the Thirty-Nine Articles, and the Augsburg
Confession. Although they differ in form (a creed
usually consists of a series of brief, succinct statements expressed as "I (we) believe"; a catechism
uses questions and answers to teach the truth; a
confession normally is a more detailed exposition
of the truth, in the remainder of this chapter I shall

---

1 Robert L. Dabney, *The Doctrinal Content of the Confession:
Its Fundamental and Regulative Ideas and the Necessity and
Value of Creeds* (Greenville, S. C.: Greenville Presbyterian
Theological Seminary, 1993), pp. 13–14.

refer to all of them by the general term "creeds."

The Biblical Basis for Creeds

Having defined what we mean by creeds, let us answer the question, "Are they biblical?" In 2 Timothy 1:13–14, God commands the use of creeds. We find here a twofold command: "Retain the standard of sound words," and "Guard the treasure entrusted to you." Many opponents of creeds argue that they detract from the sufficiency of Scripture. On the contrary, Scripture teaches us to make and use creeds.

In these two verses Paul refers, first, to the "standard of sound words." Sound words express the truths taught by Scripture. "Words" are the expression of truth that Timothy received from Paul, who was taught directly by Christ. The term "sound" means true and accurate. We use the expression, "He gave a sound diagnosis." Thus these are the doctrines that give life (1 Timothy 1:10; 6:3; 2 Timothy 4:3; Titus 2:7).[2]

Paul has communicated these to Timothy in a summary he calls "standard" or "form." The word Paul uses is a compound form of the word which we translate "type" (*tupos*; *hupotuposis*). Paul uses *tupos* in Romans 6:17: "But thanks be to God that

---

[2] George W. Knight, *Commentary on the Pastoral Epistles* (Grand Rapids, Mich.: Eerdmans, 1992), p. 89.

though you were slaves of sin, you became obedient from the heart to that *form of teaching to which you were committed*." The content of the gospel was given to them in a summary statement, a form. In 1 Timothy 1:16 he uses *hupotuposis* to mean "example." Paul says he is an "example" of one who received God's mercy and patience. In non-biblical Greek, the term is used for a sketch by a painter or architect. Moulton and Milligan's lexicon gives the meaning "sketch in outline, summary account."[3] Arndt and Gingrich say that in 2 Timothy 1:13 it means "standard".[4] Writing on verse 13, E. K. Simpson says,

> We have had *hupotuposis* in 1 Tim. 1:16. Whatever may be its precise sense there, the signification of a *summary outline*, which Galen assigns to the word, best tallies with this context. Sextus Empiricus repeatedly uses it in that acceptation. If so, it presents yet another sign that epitomes of the Christian faith were beginning to pass current. *Logoi* in the plural

---

[3] James Hope Moulton and George Milligan, *The Vocabulary of the Greek Testament* (Grand Rapids, Mich.: Eerdmans, 1974), p. 661.

[4] W. Arndt and F. Gingrich, *A Greek-English Lexicon of the New Testament and Other Early Christian Literature* (Chicago: The University of Chicago Press, 1967), p. 856.

would naturally mean *propositions* in such a connection.[5]

Thus, Paul declares that he has given to Timothy a form or pattern of apostolic doctrine. He is not referring to the entirety of his inspired corpus, but to the summary that he entrusted to Timothy.

This interpretation is reinforced in the parallel command in verse 14 when he speaks of the "entrusted treasure." In other words, this form or pattern of sound doctrine is a treasure, a specific summary that Paul has entrusted to Timothy. In 2 Timothy 2:2 he refers to this stewardship, and commands Timothy to entrust it to others: "And the things which you have heard from me in the presence of many witnesses, these entrust to faithful men, who will be able to teach others also."

Paul, therefore, refers to a summary of apostolic doctrine that he has given to Timothy. Paul describes this summary in other places as "the traditions." "Now I praise you because you remember me in everything, and hold firmly to the traditions, just as I delivered them to you" (1 Corinthians 11:2). "So then, brethren, stand firm and hold to

---

[5] E. K. Simpson, *The Pastoral Epistles: The Greek Text with Introduction and Commentary* (London: Tyndale Press, 1954), p. 127.

the traditions which you were taught, whether by word *of mouth* or by letter from us" (2 Thessalonians 2:1, cf. 3:6). Interestingly, we note here that the taught traditions were not simply those doctrines he revealed in the Epistles, but also those doctrines he taught them verbally (the summary of the apostolic message). These traditions differ from the traditions taught later by the Roman Catholic Church. Roman Catholic traditions are not summaries of biblical doctrine, but rather teachings added to the teaching of the Bible. We deny the authority of the Roman Catholic "traditions."

What Paul commands in 2 Timothy 2:13–14 is reinforced by the Bible's use of creeds. In Deuteronomy 6:4 we find the great confession, repeated to this day in the synagogue: "Hear, O Israel! The Lord is our God, the Lord is one!" Paul himself quotes two confessions. The first is in 1 Timothy 3:16: "And by common confession great is the mystery of godliness: He who was revealed in the flesh, was vindicated in the Spirit, beheld by angels, proclaimed among the nations, believed on in the world, taken up in glory." The term translated in the New American Standard Bible "common confession" literally means "confessedly," emphasizing that it was a common agreement or commitment.[6] With respect to the statement itself,

---

6 Knight, *Commentary*, p. 182.

Dr. George Knight argues that it appears to be a statement of the apostolic church, either a hymn or a creed; we cannot be certain.[7] I believe it was a creed, but even if it was a hymn Paul quotes it here as a creedal summary, common to the church.

In 2 Timothy 2:11–13, Paul gives one of his trustworthy statements: "For if we died with Him, we shall live with Him; if we endure, we shall also reign with Him; if we are faithless, He remains faithful; for He cannot deny Himself." Dr. Knight suggests that it was a creedal statement that originated in Rome:

> We can only offer a probable answer to the question of the origin of the saying. Since 2 Timothy was written from Rome, then it is possible that the church in Rome developed the first line by reflection on Romans 6 and by utilizing Rom. 6:8 in a contracted form. This is probable not only because of this link but also because the idea of dying with Christ is more fully developed in Romans 6 than anywhere else in the NT. Since Romans 6 relates death with Christ to baptism, it would be appropriate to conjecture that the saying was used in connection with confession of faith at the time of baptism. The third line seems to reflect

---

[7] *Ibid.*, pp. 182–183. cf. August Wiesnger, *Biblical Commentary on St. Paul's Epistles to the Philippians, to Titus, the First to Timothy* (Edinburgh: T&T Clark, 1858), p. 420.

Jesus' words in Mt. 10:33 and Lk. 12:9, cast here into the mold of the other lines. No very close similarity exists between the second and fourth lines and other NT statements. Thus one can only say that two likely sources have had their impact on the saying, and that the other lines were added as necessary when converts were confessing their faith and receiving baptism.[8]

We recognize, therefore, that the Bible teaches us to use creeds. We can add to the exegetical argument a number of other inferential reasons. Every Bible translation is to a degree what the translator believes the Bible teaches. By the nature of translation, no translation of the Hebrew and Greek text is neutral. Translation involves interpretation that involves faith commitments. R. L. Dabney wrote:

> All Protestants believe that Holy Scripture should be translated into the vernacular tongues of the nations. Only the Greek and Hebrew are immediately inspired; the translators must be uninspired. Therefore these ver-

---

8 Knight, *Commenting,* p. 408. For a detailed discussion see George W. Knight, *The Faithful Sayings in the Pastoral Letters* (Grand Rapids, Mich.: Baker, 1979). Dr. Knight suggests that these "faithful sayings" function also as summaries of apostolic teaching.

sions are uninspired human expositions of the divine originals. Wycliffe's version, Luther's, Tyndal's are but their human beliefs of what the Hebrew and Greek words are meant by the Holy Spirit to signify. These translators might have said with perfect truth, each one, "These renderings into English or German are my *credo*." The church which uses such a translation for the instruction of her people and the settlement of even her most cardinal doctrines is using a creed of human composition; and those who exclaim, "The Holy Scriptures themselves are our only and our sufficient creed," put themselves in a ridiculous attitude whenever they use a vernacular translation of the Scriptures, for that which they profess to hold as their creed is still but an uninspired human exposition.[10]

Furthermore, every sermon is the preacher's creed about what the text of the sermon means. The consistent consequence of "No creed but the Bible" is no preaching; just read the Scripture. But the Bible commands us to preach (2 Timothy 4:2). Again quoting Dabney:

Beyond question, God has ordained, as a means of grace and indoctrination, the oral explanation and enforcement of divine truths

---

[10] Dabney, *Doctrinal Content,* pp. 16–17.

by all preachers. Thus Ezra (Neh. 8:7) causes the priests to read in the book of the law distinctly, and give the sense, and cause them to understand the reading. Paul commanded Timothy (2 Tim. 4:2) to "reprove, rebuke, exhort with all long-suffering and doctrine." He, as an apostle of Christ, not only permits but commands each uninspired pastor and doctor to give his charge his human and uninspired expositions of what he believes to be divine truth, that is to say, his creed. If such human creeds, when composed by a single teacher and delivered orally, *extempore* [without elaborate preparation], are proper means of instruction for the church, by the stronger reason must those be proper and scriptural which are the careful, mature, and joint productions of learned and godly pastors, delivered with all the accuracy of written documents. He who would consistently banish creeds must silence all preaching and reduce the teaching of the church to the recital of the exact words of Holy Scripture without note or comment.[11]

I would add that the Church's creeds protect us from the tyranny of eccentric and heretical ideas of an individual which might be expressed in a sermon. Remember with gratitude the safety found in many counselors (Proverbs 11:14).

---

[11] *Ibid.,* p. 17.

Thus, rather than violating the sufficiency of Scripture, we see that the use of creeds is required by Scripture. Creeds do not add to the Bible, but are simply the summary of what the Church believes the Bible teaches. Thus they do not challenge the authority of the Bible. With respect to this point Samuel Miller declared:

> A church creed professes to be, as was before observed, merely an epitome, or summary exhibition, of what the Scriptures teach. It professes to be deduced from the Scriptures, and to refer to the Scriptures for the whole of its authority. Of course, when anyone subscribes it, he is so far from dishonoring the Bible that he does public homage to it. He simply declares, by a solemn act, how he understands the Bible—in other words, what doctrines he considers it as containing.[12]

The Practical Purpose of Creeds

Having determined, then, the biblical warrant for creeds, let us see what the Bible teaches about the use of creeds or their purpose. In 2 Timothy 1:13–14 we learn that the creed is to serve as an apt

---

[12] Samuel Miller, *Doctrinal Integrity: The Utility and Importance of Creeds and Confessions and Adherence to our Doctrinal Standards* (Dallas, Tex.: Presbyterian Heritage Publications, 1989), p. 30.

summary of the orthodox faith for communion and understanding. The command to "retain" means to hold, to keep as a special possession. When we hold it, it serves as our standard of communion and communication.

First, it serves as a standard for communion. One of the primary things a creed does for a church is to promote unity. Amos asks the question, "Do two men walk together unless they have made an appointment (agreement)?" We cannot walk together unless we are agreed. Think how useful it is for the congregation, and those who visit the congregation, to know what the church believes and is going to teach and preach. For this reason, the Dutch and German Reformed Churches refer to their confessional statements as "The Three Forms of Unity." The Church is not adding to the Bible, but saying, "We believe this is what the Bible teaches. If you are going to join with us you should be aware of these teachings."

In all creedal churches, the office bearers express their unity by subscribing to the doctrines agreed on in the creed. This commitment guarantees doctrinal harmony. Dabney says, "If a church is to have any honest testimony, something else is needed as a test of harmony in beliefs, a candid explanation in other terms, which, though human,

have not been misconstrued."[13] Creedal churches
do not declare that those who do not agree with
them in all these doctrines are not churches. We
recognize as true churches all those who profess
the commonly accepted doctrines of evangelical
Christianity. Again quoting Dabney,

> But we recognize as other denominations in
> the sacramental host all who teach the funda-
> mental doctrines and uphold the morals of
> Christ's gospel. We believe that the visible
> unity whereby God is to be glorified is to be
> found in the faithful recognition of each other's
> sacraments, orders and church discipline
> (limited to admonition and spiritual penalties),
> by each denomination in the church catholic;
> and not in a confusion and amalgamation of all
> into one visible ecclesiastical body; a result
> only made feasible by one or the other crimi-
> nal alternative, popery or broad churchism.[14]

Some object that the use of creeds to promote
communion actually binds the conscience, by forc-
ing people to conform. I would point out that in
Presbyterian communions individual members are
not required to subscribe to a creed. They are received on the basis of a credible profession of faith.

---

[13] Dabney, *Doctrinal Content.*, p. 20.
[14] *Ibid.*, pp. 1,16.

All who hold to the basic doctrines of the evangelical faith may be communicant members. But even here unity is protected since the church's creed makes clear what she confesses and teaches. Members will agree to expose themselves to that teaching and in no way to oppose it in the fellowship.

Furthermore, the church is a voluntary organization. We do not live in a country where we may belong only to one church. None, therefore, is bound to submit to any particular creed unless he unites with that church freely. Samuel Miller points out:

> It will not, surely, be denied by anyone, that a body of Christians have a right, in every free country, to associate and walk together upon such principles as they may choose to agree upon, not inconsistent with public order. . . . They have no right, indeed, to decide or to judge for others, nor can they compel any man to join them. But it is surely their privilege to judge for themselves, to agree upon the plan of their own association, to determine upon what principles they will receive other members into their brotherhood, and to form a set of rules which will exclude from their body those with whom they cannot walk in harmony.[15]

---

[15] Miller, *Doctrinal Integrity*, p. 3.

The creed also aids the church in the communication of the truth. This use involves both interpretation and instruction. Because they summarize the teaching of the Bible, creeds are an invaluable tool to guide in the interpretation of Scripture. Evangelical Christians believe that Scripture interprets Scripture and that the Bible does not contradict itself. Creeds, confessions and catechisms express a consensus on the major truths of the Bible. As people learn the catechism, for example, it gives them a grid by which to interpret the Bible. Westcott said, with respect to the Apostles' Creed:

> Such a summary as the Apostles' Creed serves as a clue in reading the Bible. It presents to us the salient features in the revelation which earlier experience has proved to be turning-points of spiritual knowledge. It offers centres, so to speak, round which we may group our thoughts, and to which we may refer the lessons laid open to us. It keeps us from wandering in by-paths aimlessly or at our will, not by fixing arbitrary limits to inquiry but by making the great lines along which believers have moved from the first.[16]

---

[16] Brooke Foss Westcott, *The Historic Faith: Short Lectures on the Apostles' Creed* (London: Macmillan and Co., 1893), pp. 22–23.

For example, we read in 1 Samuel that God regretted making Saul king. The immediate impression is that God had changed His mind. But the young child instructed in the Shorter Catechism definition of God knows that God is unchangeable and that His decree is irrevocable.[17] So, while not yet grasping the exact meaning of the language, even the young reader, trained in the catechism, will avoid a false interpretation.

Closely connected to interpretation is instruction. What more efficient way is there to give young Christians a compendium of the faith than by teaching them the catechisms and confessions of the church? In the Act approving the Westminster Larger Catechism, the General Assembly of the Scottish Presbyterian Church in 1648 commended this catechism as "a rich treasure for increasing knowledge among the people of God."[18] Warfield points out the educational value of the catechism in a story about D. L. Moody. When Moody was visiting a friend in London, a young man called on Moody to ask a number of questions. One had to do with prayer. He said "What is prayer? I can't tell what you mean by it!" While Moody was talking with the young man, the nine-or-ten-year-old

---

[17] Westminster Shorter Catechism, Questions 4, 7.

[18] *The Confession of Faith* (Glasgow: Free Presbyterian Publications, 1985), p. 128.

daughter of Moody's host was coming down the stairs. Her father called her and said, "Tell this gentleman what is prayer." I will let the narrator of the story tell what happened:

> Jenny did not know what had been going on, but she quite understood that she was now called upon to say her Catechism. So she drew herself up, and folded her hands in front of her, like a good little girl who was going to "say her questions," and she said in her clear childish voice: "Prayer is an offering up of our desires unto God for things agreeable to His will, in the name of Christ, with confession of our sins and thankful acknowledgement of His mercies." "Ah! That's the Catechism!" Moody said, "thank God for that Catechism."[20]

In addition to serving as an apt summary of the orthodox faith for communion and communication, creeds serve as an instrument for defending the faith. Paul commends this use in verse 14: "Guard." This is a militant term. We are vigilantly to protect and defend the truth of Scripture. Jude commands us to contend for the faith (Jude 3). The faith is under attack, and the church is entrusted

---

[20] Benjamin B. Warfield, *Selected Shorter Writings* (Nutley, N. J.: Presbyterian and Reformed Publishing Company, 1976), I:382–83.

with the responsibility of defending it. Paul says, in 1 Timothy 3:14–15, "I am writing these things to you, hoping to come to you before long; but in case I am delayed, *I write* so that you may know how one ought to conduct himself in the household of God, which is the church of the living God, the pillar and support of the truth." Part of the responsibility entailed in the Church's being a pillar and support is the defense of the truth.

For example, many of you have experienced a visit from a Mormon or Jehovah's Witness cultist, who, when asked, "Do you believe that Jesus is the Son of God?" answered, "Yes." Thus you must clarify your question. "Do you mean He is eternally God, equal with the God the Father? Do you deny that He was created?" Throughout the history of the Church creeds have served this purpose. Originally, the church developed creeds to guard against error. They continue to serve this purpose. There is no better way to expose the error of a Mormon or Jehovah's Witness than by using the question and answer of the Westminster Shorter Catechism, "Who is the Redeemer of God's elect? The only Redeemer of God's elect is the Lord Jesus Christ, who, being the eternal Son of God, became man, and so was, and continueth to be, God and man in two distinct natures, and one person, for ever."[21]

---

[21] Westminster Shorter Catechism, Q. 21.

Moreover, a believer, on the basis of the Church's creeds, may boldly say to the cultist, "Your views are a radical departure from the Christian faith."

We must guard the truth and guard the church, because false teachers will arise, "speaking perverse things, to draw away the disciples after them" (Acts 20:30).

The Spiritual Use of Creeds

Some object to the use of creeds because at times their adherents present them in an arrogant, overbearing manner. In 2 Timothy 1:13–14, Paul teaches us how to use our creeds. He commands us in verse 13 to hold the form "in the faith and love which are in Christ Jesus." Note that there should be no dichotomy between vital faith in Christ and creedal orthodoxy. If our creed is biblical, it will point us to Jesus Christ as the Savior of sinners. We will hold to our creed and express its truth in a way that acknowledges that some other sincere Christians will not agree with us on every point. We will contend for the truth while showing love for God and our neighbor. Moreover, our creeds will direct our attention to the beauty and glory of the triune God. The grand purpose of doctrine is that we might know and serve God. Thus, the church will make her confession with praise and adoration, and we will hold to our creeds and confessions evangelically. The doctrines summarized in our creeds are unto this end and we should use them accordingly.

Moreover, as we learn in verse 14, we are to hold to and guard the truth spiritually: "Guard, through the Holy Spirit." Here we learn that our creeds are not clubs to be used to cudgel others to accept our position through the power of superior intellect. We are to guard the good deposit in dependence upon the Holy Spirit. He alone will cause men and women to understand and embrace the truth we love. Paul reminds us in 2 Timothy 2:24–26 to teach the truth patiently: "And the Lord's bondservant must not be quarrelsome, but be kind to all, able to teach, patient when wronged, with gentleness correcting those who are in opposition, if perhaps God may grant them repentance leading to the knowledge of the truth, and they may come to their senses and escape from the snare of the devil, having been held captive by him to do his will."

Psalm 33:16–17 says that victory does not come through the flesh: "The king is not saved by a mighty army; a warrior is not delivered by great strength. A horse is a false hope of victory; nor does it deliver anyone by its great strength." He then reminds us that God alone is our help: "Behold, the eye of the Lord is on those who fear Him, on those who hope for His lovingkindness, to deliver their soul from death, and to keep them alive in famine. Our soul waits for the Lord; He is our help and our shield" (verses 18–20).

In summary, we have seen that God teaches the church to use creeds from a commitment to uphold and defend the faith. Creeds are a rich treasure entrusted to us. They give us a basis for communion and communication of the truths of the Bible. They protect the church and the truth entrusted to her. Rather than displacing Scripture, they are scriptural in origin and content. I count myself blessed to be a member of a confessing church that adheres to a creed which clearly sets forth the great doctrines of the historic Christian faith.

Guide me, O Thou great Jehovah,
Pilgrim through this barren land;
I am weak, but Thou art mighty;
Hold me with Thy powerful hand;
Bread of heaven, Bread of heaven,
Feed me till I want no more,
Feed me till I want no more.

William Williams

Guide Me, O Thou Great Jehovah

*John H. Gerstner on When a Person
Must Leave a Church*

When must one leave a church or a denomination? We are not asking when a person *may* leave a church or denomination, but when he or she *must* do so. We are talking here about a moral *necessity*, not a moral possibility (though some of my friends have said that I almost make moral necessity the only moral possibility!).

Before we can address ourselves to this question, we must have a working definition of a church or denomination. A church or denomination is an organized body of professed Christian believers and their children. This, I hope, will do for a working definition. Concerning children, let us simply say (bypassing all argument here) that we Presbyterians regard children of Baptists, for example, as church members, even though their denominations do not. Also, we do not mean to exclude saints in glory or the unconverted elect from the church in a certain comprehensive sense; but we are concerned here only with the church in her present militant form. It seems sufficient for our purpose to recognize the church in our context of discussion as a body of professed believers and their children.

By "believers" we mean believers in essential Christian doctrine. The Reformed churches have always drawn a distinction between essentials and non-essentials in doctrine. Since all saints are defective in character to some degree, error continues in any body of professed believers. Consequently, we do not in this world see eye to eye with God or with one another. The doctrinal unanimity which we confidently expect in heaven has not yet arrived. A doctrinal consensus on essentials, however, has arrived.

What are the essentials of Christian doctrine? Surely, they pertain to the divinity of our Lord and His saving work. Some churches would go much further in their definition of essential doctrine (unjustifiably, in my opinion); but none, to my knowledge, would fall short of this minimal definition of essentials. These may be called the essential essentials. A church, therefore, is a body of persons professing faith in the divine Lord and Savior, Jesus Christ (together with their children). Where such a professing body exists, there is a church in existence. If any group of persons, claiming the name of Christians, denies Christ's deity or His redemptive work (which is received by faith alone), that body cannot be entitled to the designation "church." On the other hand, if a body does profess such a faith as that, it must be recognized as a church regardless of how defective it may be in many other respects.

For example, a true visible church may not confess many doctrines of divine revelation. She may even oppose some non-essential, divinely revealed doctrines. Such a church may not be properly organized. She may not possess all the sacraments. She may not maintain a wholesome discipline of the membership. Standards for church offices may not be at all adequate. Nevertheless, she would meet the basic definition of a church and should be recognized as such.

This is commonplace, and yet it is of extreme importance. When discussing the question of separation from the church, we must face this prior question of the definition of the church. Manifestly, if this is a true definition, and an adequate one, it has a distinct bearing on our question, "When must one leave a church?"

Furthermore, if this is a sound definition, then all that is absolutely essential to a church is essential doctrine. We speak of the marks of the church as being the Word, the sacraments and discipline. These three surely indicate the presence of the church. When the Word, sacraments and discipline are in evidence, there a church exists. But, if our observation is correct, the absence of two of these marks (sacraments and discipline) would not belie the presence of the church. A church suffering such a twofold deficiency would not be so easily recognized and would be extremely defective. She would, nevertheless, be a church, *if* our definition is sound.

One must qualify this statement immediately. If there were no sacraments, presumably there could be a church nonetheless; but there could not be a church without organized worship. Worship is obviously implicit in the professed belief mentioned above. If a group of persons believe in Jesus Christ as the Son of God and Savior, such persons, of course, will worship Him as such. Needless to say, they should worship Him as He has prescribed in His Word. Conceivably, in their weakness, they may not worship Him properly according to His prescribed manner with and through the sacraments and public worship; but they must, nonetheless, worship Him. For example, we do not wish to deny that the evangelical Quakers are a church because they do not recognize the two traditional external sacraments while still having informal public worship nonetheless. We consider them very remiss in this deficiency, but recognize them as a church. Some would question how anyone could call himself a professed believer in Christ while refusing to observe the baptism Christ instituted, and the Lord's Supper, which He said should be taken in remembrance of Him. We do indeed consider such inconsistency a gross act of misunderstanding, but capable of happening in a highly imperfect Christian body. We should hope that evangelical Quakers would reciprocate by regarding those of us who do use external sacraments as a true church (although they must view us as being not very perceptive spiritually and sinfully defective).

Likewise, a true, though defective, church could be virtually totally lacking in discipline—virtually, but not completely. That is, such a church would have to have some conditions of admission and dismissal if a recognizable body of professing believers were to exist. A church, as we have said, would have some essentials of faith which would be the conditions of acceptance. Rejection of the same would automatically disqualify a person from membership. But, alas, all other discipline could be lacking from the body as a whole.

Inadequate discipline by a church would not exempt or prevent individual members of such a body from exercising private discipline. Thus, the Apostle Paul treated the Corinthian church as a church, even though he was shocked at their permitting an incestuous person to be in their fellowship (1 Corinthians 5:1ff). He commanded that congregation to excommunicate him, and the church did so. Meanwhile, the individuals were not told to leave that congregation, nor was that congregation denied the status of a church (1 Corinthians 1:2). The individuals were forbidden, in fact, "to associate with anyone who bears the name of brother if he is guilty of immorality or greed, or is an idolater, reveler, drunkard, or robber—not even to eat with such a one" (1 Corinthians 5:11). As individuals they were to separate themselves from such offenders, but were not to separate themselves from the church, though she was, for the time, sinfully tolerating such offenders.

We read in the post-apostolic history of the church—in the Donatist controversy of the fourth and fifth centuries, for example—of guilt by "infection." But the apostle does not hold the Corinthian church guilty by "infection," that is, by the church's tolerating an individual who should not have been tolerated. He, himself, took the initial steps to rectify the situation by commanding the congregation to proceed to discipline. The congregation did so. What we are observing here is that the church did not cease to be a church while she was delinquent in discipline; nor did the apostle require conscientious members of the church, who were offended at the presence of such an offending person, to with-

draw themselves from the church lest they be likewise contaminated.

Paul commands Timothy to avoid "godless chat-
ter, for it will lead people into more and more ungodliness, and their talk will eat its way like gan-
grene. Among whom are Hymenaeus and Philetus,
who have swerved from the truth by holding that
the resurrection is past already. They are upsetting
the faith of some." (2 Timothy 2:16–18). Here Paul
makes a very serious charge of heresy against these
two men, and indicates some of the bad effects
which are following in their congregation. Nevertheless, so far from saying that the church ceased
to exist because of the presence of such persons
unremoved, Paul continues in verse 19 and following, saying that "God's firm foundation stands,
bearing this seal: 'The Lord knows those who are
His,' and, 'let everyone who names the name of the
Lord depart from iniquity.' " Following this he gives
one of the most illuminating pictures of the visible
church which we have in the entire Bible:

> In a great house there are not only vessels of
> gold and silver, but of wood and earthenware,
> and some for noble use, some for ignoble. If
> anyone purifies himself from what is ignoble,
> then he will be a vessel for noble use, conse-
> crated and useful to the master of the house,
> ready for any good work.

How does one purify himself from that which is ignoble? The apostle had already said above that everyone who names the name of the Lord should depart from "iniquity," not from the church. Here, he follows this statement about the great house and the purifying of oneself from what is ignoble in it with this: "so shun youthful passions and aim at righteousness, faith, love, and peace, along with those who call upon the name of the Lord from a pure heart" (verse 22). Nothing is said about schism of the ecclesiastical body, but only about moral schism, that is, separation from godless chatterers, from those who have swerved from the truth, and from those who may follow youthful passions. No mention is made of separation from the church in which those persons were apparently present.

Let me summarize. The church is a body of professed believers and their children. The church exists as long as there is a sound adherence to essential Christian doctrine, even though there may be a woeful negligence in the administration of the discipline and even of the sacraments. A proper administration of the sacraments and discipline is certainly necessary to the well-being (*bene esse*) of the church, but not to the very being (*esse*) of a church. We must, in other words, be very broad in our interpretation of the *esse* of a church, very strict in our interpretation of the *bene esse*. That is, the essence of a church must be defined as broadly as possible while we must continually strive for faithful conformity to the entire revealed Word of God in doctrine, discipline and worship. This is parallel to the definition of a Christian as a person who truly believes in Christ, however poor his discipleship, and strives for perfect conformity to Him.

OBJECTION. What if this "church" is unconverted? Persons may hold essential doctrines and not be held by them. That is, they may be sound in fundamentals and not be converted. How could there be a church in such a situation, it is asked, even if such a body may meet the definition of a church which we have submitted?

ANSWER. God alone is the "Searcher of hearts." We are not able to know the spirit of a man. In a given case, we may suspect an individual, but we must give what the Puritans called a "judgment of charity." That is, we must assume that a person is what he professes to be unless there is overwhelming evidence to the contrary. Even in that case, we may not be able to remove such an offender. Meanwhile, we do not cease to have a church, for the church is not destroyed by a single offending member or many offending members.

When a "church" virtually unanimously embraces unbelief, it will feel free to admit it. Hypocrites are such only as long as it is necessary. As soon as they no longer need to dissemble, why would they do so? Thus, when trinitarian churches were being infiltrated by unitarians, the infiltrators had to dissemble and did. Once they had subverted the trinitarian churches they proudly declared their unitarianism, and still do so. This is a familiar story in the unitarian movement in New England. In trinitarian churches, unitarianism still dissembles, as is seen in the late Dr. Van Dusen's work on the new liberalism. Our point is that a church (in our definition) will never be completely corrupted under that name because there will be no need to preserve that name once it is completely corrupted.

OBJECTION. Does a church not have to declare the whole counsel of God? Does the Great Commission not require the church to teach "all that I [Christ] have commanded you" (Matthew 28:20)? That is, is the church, which is the "pillar and bulwark of the truth" (1 Timothy 3:15) not obliged to declare "the whole counsel of God" (Acts 20:27), and not merely the essential part of it? Can there be a church, therefore, which is not committed to the whole truth of God? As Cardinal Sadoleto wrote to the nascent Calvinistic church in Geneva: "Truth is always one, while falsehood is varied and multiform; that which is straight is simple, that which is crooked has many turns."

ANSWER. Indeed, a church must be committed to all that she believes God has revealed. The church will be obliged to see that those who are teachers in Israel should understand far more than those who are taught in Israel. It does not follow, however, that, because all who are proper members of the church should commit themselves to the whole counsel of God, they will all understand it to the same degree. There can be, and is, a vast difference in the comprehension of different members and officers of the one body of Christ. Our judgment is that unless a person understands so far as to comprehend the essentials of the faith, we may not recognize him as a believing member of the church. He may, however, be unable to penetrate much beyond these essentials. Such inability would not disqualify him for membership in the church. So a properly functioning church will have a double set of requirements—the first for mere members, and the second for members who are teachers of the membership. Christ's church must consist mainly of Indians. There can be very few chiefs. But Indian and chief alike belong to the same tribe. And here, in our definition of the church, we are concerned not with what distinguishes officers from other members, but with what all have alike in their profession of Christ.

As for Sadoleto and all Roman Catholics' contention that truth is one, we could not agree more. But the question is, where is that one truth to be found? We both agree that it is located in the inspired Bible. So far, so good. But the fact is that Christians interpret the non-essential elements of that one truth in many different ways. This, too, is agreed. But here comes the parting of the ways. Rome contends that there is an infallible papal interpreter of the whole counsel of God. This we dispute for many reasons, which we need not discuss here.

So we conclude that the church must declare the whole counsel of God. She does not succeed, though she must ever try. The definition of a church is not that body of Christ's disciples who succeed in this goal; that is the error of Rome which, in itself, almost disqualifies her.

So, to return to the original question, when must a person leave a church?

When a Church Ceases To Be a Church

Having developed the concept and definition of a church, we are now in a position to address the question, "When must one leave a church?" We clearly have an obligation to belong to a visible church. One obvious time to leave a visible church is when that church ceases to be a church.

Let me first emphasize this point: We must belong to a church if at all possible. That is our duty. We must therefore not separate from a church unless necessary. That too is our duty. Not to join a church is a sin of omission; to separate unnecessarily from a church is a sin of commission. These are reciprocal and inseparable sins. Not to join a church is to separate from her, and to separate from her is not to join with her. "He who is not with Me [i.e., with the church, for Christ and His body are one, Galatians 3:16] is against Me; and who is not against Me [My church] is for Me." It is true that the identity of Christ with the church refers to the mystical or invisible church; but if a person is a member of the invisible church he will endeavor to do Christ's will, which is that he be a member of a visible or organized church.

The person who is deliberately not "for" (in) the church is against Christ (the church), while that one who is not against Christ (the church) is for Christ (the church), in the sense that he is a member of the church, even though he may not recognize it. It is better, of course, that he be in it and know it. It is possible that the "mysterious miracle worker" of the gospels did not realize this. It is certain that the apostles did not. But we, instructed by Christ, should.

Surely we should never leave a church before Christ Himself requires it. If He does not separate us, we dare not separate; if He does separate us, we dare not remain. But He is far more loath to separate us than we are to separate. If Christ left us as quickly as we leave His church, many of us would be lost forever. If Christ remains faithful to us individuals who are so often faithless, ought we not to remain faithful to the church when she, too, so often proves faithless—as when she becomes our "Harlot-mother," as Samuel Rutherford called the church of Scotland, which he loved?

If, however, a "church" ceases to be a church, then those who seek the Lord God must leave. We had such a church in Northern Israel under Jeroboam. It ceased to be a church by rejecting the place which, and the personnel whom, God had appointed for His worship. Jeroboam, not wanting the Northern Israelites to go to Jerusalem and retain their ties with Judah, simply cut off the stipulated worship of Yahweh and substituted his own clergy for the priests and Levites whom God had appointed. This prevented the people of God from worshipping and professing God according to God's stipulated order. The faithful left and went where they could worship properly. 2 Chronicles 11:13–17:

> And the priests and the Levites that were in all Israel resorted to him [Rehoboam] from all places where they lived. For the Levites left

their common lands and their holdings and
came to Judah and Jerusalem, because Jeroboam and his sons cast them out from serving as priests of the Lord, and he appointed his
own priests for the high places, and for the
satyrs, and for the calves which he had made.
And those who had set their hearts to seek the
Lord God of Israel came after them from all the
tribes of Israel to Jerusalem to sacrifice to the
Lord, the God of their fathers. They strength-
ened the kingdom of Judah, and for three years
they made Rehoboam the son of Solomon secure, for they walked for three years in the
way of David and Solomon.

No place or order is so sacrosanct today. But if a
church were forbidden to assemble herself and to
worship the living God through Jesus Christ, she
could do nothing but refuse to continue under such
circumstances. The faithful would have to separate
not from the church, but from that body which
falsely called itself a church. This is the lesson we
learn from 2 Chronicles 13:11ff. If the faithful had
not been able to flee, what then? Presumably, they
would not have bowed the knee to Baals, and may
have been obliged, for a time, to exist without corporate worship—a situation to be corrected at the
first opportunity. Meanwhile, like Daniel in Baby-
lon, the faithful would have openly worshipped the
true God, even though alone and separately. Thus

the church would continue visible, though fragmented into her individual members.

Something equally drastic is represented in the New Testament in 2 Corinthians 6:14–18:

> Do not be mismated with unbelievers. For what partnership have righteousness and iniquity? Or what fellowship has light with darkness? What accord has Christ with Belial? Or what has a believer in common with an unbeliever? What agreement has the temple of God with idols? For we are the temple of the living God; as God said, "I will live in them and move among them, and I will be their God and they shall be My people. Therefore, come out from them and be separate from them," says the Lord, "and touch nothing unclean; then I will welcome you, and I will be a Father to you, and you shall be My sons and daughters," says the Lord Almighty.

We do not know all the circumstances of the apostle's command here. Obviously, Christians are forbidden to be united (mismated) with avowedly non- and anti-Christians. Whether Paul was alluding to some group which had once professed the name of Christ, and had broken off and was now committed to the worship of idols (Belial), we do not know. If he was, he was forbidding the true church at Corinth to be associated with them. They were to come apart and be separate. This is obviously a reference to some kind of worship and not merely to secularity ("what agreement has the temple of God with idols?"). Paul has taught us elsewhere that we are not to break off relationships with the "fornicators of the world" because, in order to do so, we would have to go out of this world (1 Corinthians 5:10). Business and social relations could continue with the children of this world no matter how wicked they may be. However, we could never join with them in worship. What we have here is a command not that the faithful should separate from the church, but that the church should separate herself from the sinful worship of the world. The church is never to separate from herself. She is never, on the other hand, to be in union with the world in actual worship (mismated with unbelievers).

A question may arise about the Galatians. Paul addresses them as the "church of Galatia" (Galatians 1:2), but, at the same time, feels that they have apostatized. They began in the Spirit, and they wanted to perfect themselves in the flesh (3:3). They were listening to false teachers of another gospel, which was not a gospel, and whose teachers Paul anathematized (1:9, 5:12). The apostle was obviously greatly exercised with the doctrinal delinquency of the Galatians, who seemed certainly to be repudiating essential faith in the divine Lord and only Savior (2:16–21). Yet Paul does not separate from them, nor call the faithful members within them to separate from the delinquent members.

Does this not seem to militate against our principle that a church cannot exist where the very fundamentals of the faith are being denied? I think that in the case of the Galatians we have not reached the bottom line. That is, the Galatians are foolish and bewitched (3:1), and they are being warned by the apostle. However, it is not yet clear that they have finally apostatized. Certainly Paul is pleading with them to turn away from the path on which they seem to have embarked. Had they really committed themselves to another gospel? If so, would Paul not have said somewhere in his epistle that true believers must not be unequally yoked together with these Galatians? He does not do this. What must be concluded? It seems that the apostle is still pleading, urging, and warning, but also waiting to see whether the foolish Galatians will wise up, whether these bewitched ones will come out of their trance. He is not yet persuaded, apparently, that they have abandoned the faith, though they are looking in that direction. He speaks to the Galatians as Christ does to the church in Sardis, calling it "on the point of death" (Revelation 3:2).

He is warning them rather than writing them off. He is pleading with them rather than turning away from them as he did with the Jewish persons in Antioch: "Since you thrust it [the Word of God] from you, and judge yourselves unworthy of eternal life, behold, we turn to the Gentiles" (Acts 13:46; cf. 18:6, 28:28).

I think we have something here analogous to the experience of the church in relationship to the incarnate Christ. "He came to His own, and His own received Him not" (John 1:11). But He did not reject them; they rejected Him. They crucified Him, yet still He did not reject them. In His name, the Apostle Peter, at Pentecost, called them to repent and believe on their Christ. The apostles continued to worship in the temple. Even Paul, the apostle to the Gentiles, in the beginning went first to the synagogue to present Christ to his own kinsmen after the flesh. In other words, though the Jewish church was acting as the Galatian church was later to act, she was not regarded as having yet finally apostatized. The apostles continued to witness to her and plead with her. Many of her members were won to Jesus Christ. Only when it was obvious that the Jews generally would remain unbelieving and refuse to hear the gospel any longer did the apostles turn away.

Did the apostles turn away from a church? Did

they separate from a church? No, they separated
from an unbelieving body of people. This is clearly
implied in the words which follow the earlier reference to Paul's turning away from the synagogue at
Antioch: "Since you thrust it from you, and judge
yourselves unworthy of eternal life, behold, we turn
to the Gentiles. For so the Lord has commanded us,
saying, 'I have set you to be a light for the Gentiles,
that you may bring salvation to the uttermost parts
of the earth.' And when the Gentiles heard this,
they were glad and glorified the word of God; and
as many as were ordained to eternal life believed"
(Acts 13:46–48).

Another objection may arise here from the opposite direction. We have just considered the objection that Paul did not separate even when the
Galatians were tempted not to be a true church. We
have answered that; but now we hear someone saying that the Reformers separated though the
Roman Catholic Church had not ceased to be a
true church. That is, the Rome of the sixteenth century, from which the Reformers separated, professed to believe in the divine Christ and His substitutionary atonement. Rome even went so far as to
believe that faith in Him and His sacrifices was
necessary to salvation. Nevertheless, the Reformers
separated from that "church," and not only Martin
Luther when he was driven out, but John Calvin

and others who went out. In 1544 Calvin wrote his *Necessity of Reforming the Church.* For Calvin, "reforming" meant separating and separating now.

So the question is, who is wrong here? According to John Gerstner's principles, John Calvin should never have separated and John Gerstner should not be in John Calvin's church. No, John Calvin should have separated and John Gerstner has a right to be in his church; but it does need some explaining. The fact is that, according to Calvin, the Roman church, though it professed faith in Christ's atonement and His doctrine, nevertheless rejected the essential doctrine of justification by faith alone, not to mention essentially corrupting the worship and discipline of the church. For Calvin, justification by faith alone was the "hinge of the Reformation." That Rome had repudiated that doctrine he showed in his tract. Calvin explained that there were "defects which the pious are indeed bound to disapprove, but which are to be borne with." The situation was far more serious than that. He argued: "The doctrine of salvation was entangled with such numerous destructive errors . . . that the virtue of Christ's death was suppressed." The Church of Rome was teaching men to procure eternal life by the merit of their own works.

It should be noted incidentally, even here, how

concerned Calvin was to avoid schism. We are, he insists, "to beware of separating the church from Christ its head" (p. 141). But on the other hand, the Reformer warns, "It is not enough simply to throw out the name of church, but judgment must be used to ascertain which is the true church, and what is the nature of its unity" (p. 140). Earlier, he had indicated the same thing in his answer to the letter of Cardinal Sadoleto. In this classic response he grounds his separation on Rome's rejection of justification: "Wherever the knowledge of it is taken away, the glory of Christ is extinguished, religion abolished, the Church destroyed, and the hope of salvation utterly overthrown" (p. 66). These are our sentiments exactly. Rome had denied the essential doctrine and ceased to be a true church. She had separated from us.

Although, therefore, the Roman church had preserved a very great deal of the truth of Holy Scripture, including some of the essentials of Christian doctrine, she had rejected indispensable elements as well. It is essential not only to affirm that Christ is divine and His sacrifice vicarious, but that it is the sole sacrifice, and altogether sufficient for the salvation of the individual who appropriates it by a non-meritorious faith. To deny the latter truth is to make the former truths fail to constitute a church. This is what Luther had in mind when he declared that justification by faith alone is the "article by which the Church stands or falls." Without *sola fide* there can be no *sola gratia*. Justification by faith alone is essential to the doctrine of salvation by Christ alone (Romans 4:16). Though there were many other errors charged to Rome, this was the crucial one in the minds of the Reformers. Furthermore, Rome's doctrines of the sacrifice of the Mass, transubstantiation, and intercession and adoration of the saints and the "Blessed Virgin," combined with the recognition of *ex opere operato* sacraments destroyed an acceptable Christian worship, according to the Reformers.

We have attempted to show that when a professing church has repudiated essential truth we must separate from it because it is no longer the body of Christ, but merely a corpse. We now turn to the only other reason for separation.

When a Church Requires Us To Deny What We Believe or Believe What We Deny

The first reason for separating from a church is the church's denial of essential doctrine, by which it ceases to be a church. The second reason is a church's demanding that we deny non-essential doctrine which we believe. It does not matter how non-essential the doctrine may be—if an individual believes it, it is essential that he continue to do so.

It is essential that he be loyal, even to non-essential doctrine. He must not require this non-essential doctrine, or even desire that a church require it. He should, however, require a church not to require him to disavow it.

Likewise, a church may not require us to believe what we deny. According to the Scripture, "whatsoever is not of faith is sin" (Romans 14:23). To affirm, therefore, what we do not have faith in is to sin. No church may require us to do that. We must obey God (as we understand Him) rather than man (church). Eating meat offered to idols was not in itself sinful, the apostle clearly teaches. Nevertheless, the "weaker brother" who thought it was sinful was required to abstain from it, and the stronger brother was required to abstain from urging the younger brother to overcome his scruples (Romans 14:13ff).

We have many instances in history of a church attempting to impose such non-essentials, and thereby causing trouble in the church. What once disturbed the old United Presbyterian Church concerned the inability and unwillingness of some persons to ordain women. No one, but no one taught that it was essential to the Christian religion that women be ordained. No one would be prepared to say that this is an article by which the church stands or falls. The U. P. church was, in some of her presbyteries, barring men from ordination for an unwillingness to consent to the ordination of women; but she had not yet attempted to bar anyone from membership in the church for that reason. That would have forced those persons to leave that church who simply could not and would not affirm what they could not believe.

Presbyterians were divided at the time of the Civil War not because of the slavery issue, but because of another matter. The issue which separated the two geographical parts of the Presbyterian Church into two separate denominations was the insistence of the General Assembly that everyone in our church was obliged to be in agreement with the civil government. This was a strange position, indeed, coming from an American church which had almost uniformly rejected the authority of the British government one hundred years earlier. But because the Northern part of our church imposed this regulation on the dissenting Southerners, they were driven out of the denomination on an issue which should not have been imposed. But believing that their section of the country was justified in rebelling against the other section of the country, they adhered to their confederate government and were removed from the denomination for this theologically non-essential matter. If our church had not imposed this doctrine on a part of her constituency, the Presbyterian church may have been able to survive the schism in the country (as the Anglicans and the Roman Catholics were able to do), and remain an undivided church in a subsequently reunited country. But our Southern brethren were forced to separate because they had to accept a non-essential doctrine. We repeat: what is essential in the Christian religion is for any individual or group of individuals to hold what they believe to be true.

Consider the Covenanters. They believe in unaccompanied, exclusive Psalm-singing in public worship. Is such a doctrine essential to the Christian religion? Even the Covenanters themselves do not think so. That is, they believe that other Christians who use musical accompaniment to their hymns are still worshipping the true and living God. We do not become, in their opinion, a synagogue of Satan because we do not worship God in the manner they believe to be required by Scripture. Very well; ideally both of us should bear and forbear on this matter. They should be permitted who are of such a mind to worship in that particular manner. They should not be cut off from us because they do not worship as the majority of us are inclined to worship. But should they cut us off from them because they do not worship as the majority of us are inclined to worship? Should they cut us off from

them because we cannot see the necessity of worshipping as they do? We think not. It would be
well if we could all agree, but is it necessary that
we all agree? Definitely not, so long as one group
does not attempt to impose its will in this non-essential matter on the other group. We should not
make otherwise-minded Christians sing hymns,
and they should not require us to sing Psalms ex-
clusively.

Consider, by contrast, the Covenanter practice of
closed communion. Covenanters cannot admit to
their administration of the Lord's Supper any who
are not in conformity with their doctrine and practice. What do we say about this? This is quite different from the matter of exclusive psalmody,
which is (in our majority opinion) a non-essential
error. This, however, is an error in essentials. The
Lord's Table is for all Christ's children. The
Covenanter practice bars some of His children from
it, and that cannot be tolerated. There is nothing
that the Covenanters can do but practice according
to their conscientiously held doctrine. On the other
hand, there is nothing we can do but oppose them
resolutely, even though it involves a separation, because they have made non-essential doctrine (their
total Reformed system) into an essential doctrine
(that is necessary for communion). When the
Covenanters come into non-Covenanter services,

they may worship with us except at the point of singing, from which they must abstain in accordance with their conscience. But they can pray with us, worship with us, listen to the Word of God with us, offer their sacrifices of gifts and praise with us, and break bread with us. It is not essential that they should participate in the singing, even though it is lamentable that they cannot. It is essential that they be admitted to our Table, and that we be admitted to their Table, because that Table is neither ours nor theirs, but the Lord's. The Table of the Lord is for all His children. No church dares bar any who are not under discipline. They are admitted to our administration, but we are barred from theirs. To bar us is to imply that we are not the Lord's children. They may not mean to do that, but what other implication can there be? If it is the Lord's Table and we are the Lord's children, why are we barred? If we submitted to this discrimination we would be saying that we are not believers in Christ. This we cannot do. We are obliged to confess Christ by separation because they require us to believe what we deny, namely that acceptance of the entire Reformed system (as Covenanters understand it) is essential to admission to the Lord's Table.

Supposing we have correctly argued that the only two conditions for separation from a church are (first) when a church ceases to be a church by rejecting essential Christianity, or (second) when a church requires a member, contrary to his own conviction, to believe some non-essential doctrine or practice. Let me apply this position to two problems which some mainline denominations have faced, and continue to face: the ordination of women and the ordination of homosexuals. The former has been authorized by the mainline Presbyterian denomination since 1930; the latter is not yet authorized. The former is approved probably by an overwhelming majority of church members, including conservatives. The latter is approved (probably) by a minority of church members, and disapproved by virtually all conservatives. The former does not concern the ordination of women, but the toleration of officers who, though willing to work with ordained women, cannot approve their ordination. The latter is concerned with not just the ordination of homosexuals, but also the consistency of homosexuality with Christian faith.

The Ordination of Women Issue

If a person is unable to approve the ordination of women, and is therefore barred from ordination himself, does this justify separation? Even this does not require separation. Neither the ordination of women, nor the non-ordination of those who are against the ordination of women, can justify separation. Whether we think a church errs in ordaining women and/or errs in not ordaining men who will not ordain women, we regard either of these errors, serious as they may be, as non-essential, and therefore as not justifying separation.

Of course men who are thus debarred from ordination may consider seeking ordination where it may be had. We would say that that is not morally necessary unless a person feels absolutely persuaded that he must go into the ordained ministry. Since God no longer especially calls persons by supernatural revelation into the ministry, we doubt if anyone can be so certain of his calling that he cannot suffer deprivation in this case. Since there are other denominations which are opposed to the ordination of women, making this person's ordination possible, these options may, no doubt, appeal to him. He is not *required* to leave, but *may* he leave?

A prior question is whether that other denomination has an excuse for its own existence. This tends to become academic since so many denominations have, in fact, existed for centuries. It is no longer possible for the average person to find out the original justification, or claim to justification, of many denominations. They are simply accepted as

facts of ecclesiastical life. If this other denomination is thus accepted as legitimately existing, then,
of course, a person (who cannot be ordained in his
own denomination) may feel authorized to go into
this other denomination without creating any further denominational separation. He would be simply seeking for a more adequate sphere of ministry
than his own denomination affords him at the present. But once again we are reminded of the principle that "This is the curse of evil deed: that of
new evil it becomes a seed." That is, a denomination which originally may never have been justified
in its formation is accepted because of merely existing in time. If it were not accepted, and if it did not
exist as another denomination, the person who
cannot be ordained would not be able to enter it, or
even leave his own without causing an unnecessary
separation.

Let us focus more clearly on that last point.
Suppose there was only one evangelical and reformed denomination in the country. Suppose this
denomination not only ordained women, but required men who would be ordained to approve of
the ordination of women. Would a man who could
not thus approve, and, therefore, was barred from
ordination, be justified in attempting to create a
denomination in which he could be ordained? We
think not, even though he would be deprived of a

deserved ordination. He could suffer for what he deemed to be righteousness' sake, and thereby show his love for his erring brothers and sisters. He could teach in some lay capacity and certainly teach us all by his forbearance.

It seems that all we can say at this point (since many different denominations do in fact exist, and there is virtually no prospect of dissolving many, or perhaps any, of them) is what has been said before: A person *ought not* to separate from a denomination on the basis of a non-essential such as the ordination of women.

The Ordination of Homosexuals Issue

Now let us face the question of the homosexual in the church. Let it be noted at the outset that when we talk about homosexuals in the church, we talk about persons who are avowed, impenitent, practicing homosexuals. These are individuals who consider this a legitimate way of life. Note also that we are talking about homosexuals in the church, not necessarily in the ministry of the church. The question is before some churches at the level of the ordination of homosexuals, but the problem exists whether ordination is discussed or not. Those who oppose it do so because they believe the Bible forbids homosexuality in *any* of its members, not merely ministers. The ordination of homosexuals, therefore, is only an extension of the fundamental issue.

What, then, about homosexuals in the church? Suppose that the church does permit homosexuals in the membership and the ministry. What are we to do? Does this require or permit separation by way of protest?

First of all, the biblical question must be answered. Until recently it was not doubted that the Bible forbade homosexuality. However, it is questioned today by some (few) serious biblical expositors. Whenever anyone questions the biblical fidelity of the church's traditional practice, she must respond. Unless she deems herself to be an infallible interpreter of the Bible (which the Protestant church does not), she must respond respectfully to any such challenges to her interpretation. Some are raising the homosexual question at the present time.

Suppose that the church actually comes to endorse the homosexual lifestyle in its members and/or ministers. Suppose that, at the same time, some of us, many of us, most of us, or all of us remain of our present persusasion that the Bible does not condone this practice in members, not to mention ministers. What then? Well, we will be in disagreement with our church. We cannot profess to agree with what we do not agree with. If our membership or ordination depended upon complete agreement with the official position (as in the Roman Catholic Church), we would have to forfeit either or both. If our church were to take the position that, when a person affirms and endorses his church's government, he thereby and therein endorses the legitimacy of the ordination and membership of homosexuals, we could not do that. We would have to refuse and take whatever consequences are forthcoming, whether it be the preventing of ordination or removal of ordination. Our church (in such a case) would be wrong, we believe, in taking such action. She would be opposing a person for something which was not an offense, namely the disapproval of homosexuality.

We realize that this is very difficult for some to read. You are utterly convinced that homosexuality, not opposition to homosexuality, is the sin. I am speaking here, however, of the situation if the church came to regard homosexuality as legitimate, and what that would do to your relationship to such a church. You would be found offending because you took a position against homosexuality. I am simply observing here that your offense (from the church's standpoint) should be considered minor and not essential. The church should not proceed to discipline you, even from the church's own (hypothetical) viewpoint.

But the more serious question for persons who are opposed (and remain opposed) to homosexual legitimacy is not whether the church should tolerate them, but whether they should tolerate such a church. Admittedly, recognizing homosexuality would be a very great blemish on the church. If we believe that the Bible forbids homosexuality and indicates that homosexuals (avowed, impenitent, practicing homosexuals) cannot inherit the Kingdom of God (1 Corinthians 6:9), we cannot help but weep at the thought of our church saying otherwise. In this regard, she would be not the pillar and bulwark of the truth (1 Timothy 3:15), but the pillar and bulwark of falsehood—damnable falsehood. But would she cease to be a church? Certainly not a church without blemish, but would she cease to be a church? We think not. If she does not cease to be a church, could we cease to be a member of her? If she cannot be shown to have forsaken Christ (even though in this regard she has disobeyed Christ), can we forsake her?

We would find ourselves in a very strange situation. We could not privately associate with a person with whom we would be required publicly and ecclesiastically to associate. That is, we may have to administer the Lord's Supper with a homosexual man or woman on the session. We may have to be subordinate to homosexual moderators of presbytery or higher courts. Nevertheless, we could neither approve of them as Christian, nor have the slightest hope of their salvation, while they remain impenitent. How could such an anomalous situation as that be tolerated?

I refer again to Paul, who wrote: "But rather I wrote to you not to associate with anyone who bears the name of brother if he is guilty of immorality or greed . . . not even to eat with such a one" (1 Corinthians 5:11). The apostle here is speaking of an immoral brother. Such persons ought to be disciplined, but these Corinthian offenders are not. Christ teaches us that even an unforgiving person ought to be excommunicated and treated as a heathen and a tax collector (Matthew 18:15–18). Here the apostle (who certainly would not disagree with his Lord) is, at the same time, acknowledging that someone worse than an unforgiving person might yet still be called a "brother." We are required by the apostle to show our disapproval of the immorality of such brethren—and to show it in a most drastic manner—by refusing to eat with them; that is, by refusing to have any ordinary social fellowship with them. We are sure that 2 John has the same spirit in mind when it speaks about that immorality called heresy, and says that we should not even give heretical persons a greeting (v. 10). But the point here is that they may be called brethren, and, presumably, even officers.

Our church may not permit us to behave in the prescribed apostolic manner. She may insist that we must treat these brothers and sisters, who are immoral in our view, without discrimination. She may censure us as being unchristian in our attitude and discipline *us*! We may not separate from her. She may, on the other hand, separate us and remove us. Then (when she casts us off), and then only, may we separate from her until she repents of her uncharitable error and receives us again into her bosom.

Conclusion

Finally, granted that separation tends to obscure the unity of the church, you may ask, does it not sometimes promote her purity? It certainly does not promote the purity of the church from which one separates because of impurity. The separatist is only abandoning her to greater impurity. Is it promoting the purity of the body to which he goes? If a person has broken the charity of the church by leaving unnecessarily, has he not also embodied an impure doctrine? Can he separate unnecessarily without being impure in the doctrine of the church? The right to unjustified separation is an error in doctrine which also leads to schism in action; first of all, though, it is an error in doctrine. "Heresy" in

Galatians is factiousness (5:20). The heretic is a factious person, and the factious person is a heretic. So schism is a blemish on both the unity and the purity of the church. "To him that hath not [charity] shall be taken even that which he hath [purity]."